ABOUT THE AUTHORS

Ram Gidoomal is a successful Asian businessman who took early retirement at the age of 40 to concentrate full-time upon charitable activities. He is a director of SOLOTEC (the South London Training and Enterprise Council) and business advisor to the Prince's Youth Business Trust. He is also chairman of Christmas Cracker; a trustee of the Oasis Trust; director of South Asian Concern; and on the councils of a number of other bodies. He is the co-author of *Loving Your Hindu Neighbour*.

Mike Fearon is a professional writer, working in an urban London borough where half the population is of Asian origin, and one in four have been the subject of racial attacks. He is the publications director of Network Information Limited; editor of *New Consciousness* magazine; secretary to ELCHAHA (East London Churches Housing and Homelessness Alliance); he serves on the management committees of several charities; he is a popular public speaker and broadcaster; and a regular contributor to many magazines and newspapers. His other books include: *Devils's Island* (with Jimmy Murphy), *Martin Luther: The Man Who Lived in Fear*, *Youth in the City* (with Peter Stow), *With God on the Frontiers*, and *No Place Like Home*.

SARI 'N' CHIPS

SARI 'N' CHIPS

Ram Gidoomal
with Mike Fearon

MARC
South Asian Concern

First published 1993
Reprinted 1993

ISBN 1 85424 225 3

Unless otherwise indicated, biblical quotations are from the
New International Version © 1973, 1978, 1984 by the
International Bible Society.

Co-published with South Asian Concern,
P.O. Box 43, Sutton, Surrey SM2 5WL

Production and Printing in England for
MARC, an imprint of Monarch Publications,
P.O. Box 163, Tunbridge Wells, Kent TN3 0NZ
by Nuprint Ltd, Harpenden, Herts AL5 4SE.

ACKNOWLEDGEMENTS

Many people have helped in the preparation of this book. I would particularly like to thank:

Mike Fearon for his help with research and writing.

Tony and Jane Collins for their creative input and ideas.

Dr Raju Abraham and Prabhu Guptara for encouraging me to pursue this project.

Friends at Westlake and EBGC (Switzerland), Crossroads (France) and in Perth (Scotland).

My mother (Vasanti), my aunt (Janki), my mother in law (Vishni) and members of my extended family—all of whom I dearly love and do not meet as frequently as I would like (because of undertaking projects like this book!).

My prayer support group—Prof. D. J. Wiseman, Peter Morris, Chris Lee, Brian Adams, Roy Coad and my fellow elders, members and friends at Chiltern for praying this project through.

My children Ravi, Nina and Ricki, and last but not least my wife Sunita—without whose help I would not have completed this project.

Dedicated to all immigrants, refugees and ethnic minority groups wherever they may be.

'The Lord watches over the immigrant, and sustains the fatherless and the widow.'

(The Book of Psalms—Psalm 146.)

CONTENTS

FOREWORD

By Contessa Bina Sella di Monteluce (née Bina Indurkumar Shivdasani)

MUST ASIANS IN THE WEST lose their cultural identity? The question is so subtle and multi-layered that it can often take many years for an Asian to recognise that there is even a problem, and then a whole lifetime to adequately resolve it.

For myself, I was born in India at about the same time that India herself was born as an independent nation. I arrived in Britain at eleven months old, and was immediately whisked off by my father to a pub, where he was meeting some chums. I was unceremoniously sat on the bar and within minutes I had produced a frothy puddle of my own.

The experience quite acclimatised me to Britain—though my early years were spent travelling around Europe with my father. He took me everywhere with him: into his board meetings with Swiss bankers, to the *Folies Bergères* and *Maxims* in Paris, to the Côte d'Azur and so on.

Father originally came to Europe after grandfather insisted that he study at Cambridge, saying, 'Britain is a tiny island with very few people, compared to India. But it managed to build the largest empire the world has ever seen, upon which the sun never set. You'd better go there and learn some empire-building skills!' The experience was the founding of his global business empire.

When I reached the age of five, someone suggested to him

11

that perhaps he ought to send me to school. The idea had never previously occurred to him, but it led to him purchasing his first home in Britain, and sending me to schools first in Wimbledon and then Cheltenham.

Though occasionally my school friends had been intrigued by my hair and skin colour, which they perceived as being different from their own, it was at boarding school that I first became aware of the odd attitudes that some people have about Asians. Some of the other girls asked me if we all lived in mud huts! Asians were a rarity in Britain at that time, and many westerners thought of India as being like a place out of the Bible, rather than a bustling modern country. When I explained this to my school friends there were no more problems. In those early sixties, there was much less sense of racial tension. Because there were so few of us, we were easily and happily absorbed. My friends and I were very liberal, and opposed to any form of racial facism.

For me, the period in my life where I felt strong conflict between my Indian background and the western lifestyle exploding around me was after I left school and moved to London. For about a year I struggled to find some sense of my own identity. Mixing with people of all nationalities, it was apparent that western values were different from Asian values, particularly regarding dating and sexual morality. My close girlfriends were the English girls with whom I had been to school. When I met other Asian girls, I started to think, gosh, to which culture do I belong?

Right from the beginning, my father was very much a world traveller, who considered himself a global citizen, rather than attached to one country. Like him, I eventually came to realise that there is a deeper reality beyond all of us, which is more important than ties of culture or background.

Because my parents are very liberal, I wasn't expected to have an arranged marriage. But when my parents went to Rome to meet the father of my Italian boyfriend, whom I was going to marry, they got so excited that they rang us up in India to tell us that they had *arranged* our engagement. We had a Latin Mass in the Jesuit church in Farm Street and got a special dispensation from Rome to have the Vedic wedding also in the church. How's that for a mix of cultures?

When my son was four years old, he came from his pre-prep school and said to me, 'Mummy, it's too muddling being half and half. I don't want to be half Indian and half European, it's too confusing. I've decided that I would like to be whole.' I asked him which whole he would like to be: Eastern or Western. He said, 'No, mummy, I've decided to be whole American, and I'm going to be that football player, The Refrigerator.'

It's wonderful about the new generation of western Asians that my son, who could decide to be white or pale brown, decided instead to be a black 300 pound Afro-Caribbean!

I truly believe that the conflicts which many Asians living in the west are feeling about their personal identity—are they Asians or Westerners?—represent a passing phase. Young Asians these days are very caring, very spiritual, and very open to new developments. How long before Asian restaurants start serving Tandoori chips? Fashion designer Zandra Rhodes has already started designing dresses which look like saris; perhaps before too long on the beaches of St Tropez, instead of being topless, the women will all be wearing mini-saris!

We've had the agricultural age and the industrial age, and now we have the age of communication. World wide, women always worry about their children, their home and their menfolk. It's the same the world over. In India, America or Europe, young people are watching the same programmes on satellite television, and MTV looks the same wherever you are. Cross-cultural music is taking off in a way which makes the world seem to shrink faster into a great global village.

I'm a tremendous optimist, and I feel that the world's current travails are only a temporary stage. There is a huge battle taking place as people of all cultures struggle for meaning, and discover where the world is heading. But a new and far better age is dawning.

Some of the stories in this book may make painful reading, but they are targeted at helping people through this difficult stage of transition, and all the crises it brings with it. The book explores how East and West can be fully reconciled, while remaining faithful to both cultures. I commend it to you.

(Bina Sella is a successful Asian businesswoman involved in commercial real estate in the United States of America.)

PREFACE

THERE WILL BE SOME SOUTH ASIANS who will read this book in disgust and disbelief. 'All lies!' they will say. 'There is *no* crisis in Asian families, and no difficulties in adjusting to western society. I have never experienced the severity of the problems described here.'

Sadly, there will be other Asians who shake their heads for a very different reason. 'This is all soft soap,' they will say. I have experienced much worse difficulties than these!'

There's no pleasing everybody, and this would be a far duller world if everyone was exactly alike. We can celebrate our varied opinions and experiences—our differences of colour and culture—*only* if we tolerate the views of those with whom we are in disagreement. If we can't learn to love our enemies and respect views that are different from our own, then we are ourselves no better than the bigots whose prejudices we suffer and decry.

There can't be many South Asians who have undergone *all* the tribulations described in these pages, but few will have completely escaped them all. Ram Gidoomal and I pray that many Asians will benefit from the knowledge that they are not alone in the difficulties they face, and that—as others have found—it is possible to overcome the problems and setbacks, and to end up enriched by the experience of handling adversity.

But this is not a book *just* for Asians. It is our belief that

15

many westerners will benefit from the insight it gives into a different, and often exotic, culture. If this book makes the ways of their Asian neighbours and friends look a little less inscrutable to western eyes, then it will have served a dual purpose.

Though describing mainly the difficulties faced by those Asians whose ultimate place of origin is on the Indian sub-continent and its immediate surrounds—defined as South Asia—many of the problems will be familiar to those from South-East Asia, China, or even the Middle-East.

In putting this volume together, Ram and I are grateful for the assistance of Prabhu Guptara, June George, Sunita Gidoomal, Vishal Mangalwadi, Rona Taylor, Tara Singh, Bina Sella, Sue Barley, Raju Abraham, Sheena Gidoomal and Tony Collins; and to the work of other researchers and writers too numerous to mention here, but whose names and works appear in the Bibliography.

Every blessing.

Mike Fearon
Newham
February 1993

INTRODUCTION

I T'S AN EVERYDAY STORY of boy meets girl! The boy is
Asian with matinee idol looks—a graduate of Westminster
School and America's prestigious Wharton Business
School. He is described as 'a very good student, well-liked and
well-mannered.' He has fantastic cars and wears top-of-the-line
clothes, bought for him by his doting father. His father is one of
the richest men in the world, who wants nothing but the best for
his only son. The boy is described as having qualities of consideration and modesty, a mind and a heart.

The girl is beautiful with a strongly western outlook, the
youngest of eleven children born to her Indian mother...and
Jewish father! She is a half-caste, or *chichis*, and despite the
boy's wholly western upbringing, his father is part of a closely-
knit, conservative Hindu family who wants nothing but an
arranged marriage for his son, who is said to be kept on too
tight a leash and expected to be 'more Indian than the Indians.'

Of different class, colour and creed, they first meet in Bombay, and then (it's believed) secretly in locations across the
globe. The star-crossed lovers are secretly married in Chelsea
Registry Office, with only two London friends as witnesses, and
their doom is sealed. To shake off the boy's family, the couple
fake a kidnapping in India; lay a false trail in Mauritius; and
even fake his death in a burnt out car outside Bombay.

17

Their marriage only four months old, the couple are trapped in their bolt hole, a cheap back-street hotel in Mauritius where the boy has checked in well-disguised and under an assumed name, and wait for the inevitable. His family have discovered the boy's name on an Air India flight out of Bombay, and— aunts, uncles and all—have established their headquarters nearby at the exclusive Royal Palm Court hotel, from where they have made contact with the local media.

The boy sees his photograph in the morning paper and knows that discovery and disgrace are only hours away. He buys a bottle of paint thinner, pours it over himself, and lights the fateful match.

Like a human torch, screaming in agony, he staggers into the corridor where hotel staff extinguish the blaze which covers 75% of his body, and rush him to hospital, his new wife crying 'I love you.'

Hours later, he is reunited in a burns unit with his distraught father, who arranges for him to be flown to London to receive the best treatment money can buy. *He reveres his father, but loves the girl.* In Queen Mary's Hospital, Roehampton, the toxins produced by his injuries make surgery inevitable, his kidneys fail, and finally his respiratory system. The golden boy, who had everything to live for, is dead.

What a tragedy! I could hardly believe it as I read the story in my Sunday newspaper on quiet afternoon in my Surrey home with my own Asian family.

It doesn't matter who the boy was. Rich or poor, high caste or low caste, such tragedies are increasing as young Asians are pulled by pressures from different quarters. Punjabis wishing to marry Gujeratis, girls wishing to pursue careers against the wishes of their parents, boys increasingly adopting western values, and ignoring the expectations of their community. Such situations inevitably lead to conflict. In this extreme case, the east-west tensions cost the family their beloved son.

Not every story has such a tragic ending. But will families study the lesons of these crises, lessons that confront the growing number of Asians living in foreign environments: How are they going to treat their children of marriagable age? Are they going to push them into a corner? Or are they going to talk to them so that they are not driven into such awful actions?

That's the kind of question which a lot of Asian families are going to have to face up to in the years ahead.

Today, many Asian families—whether new immigrants or second generation Asians born in the west—are facing a crisis of identity. In the home, they are part of the Asian culture, doing things in the Asian way. But at school or work they are presented with the local western culture. This often causes terrible conflicts, and loss of identity.

Asians Abroad

The popular western conception of India, which preceded immigration, was of 'a land of teeming millions, of filth and squalor, of exotic and peculiar customs'. Peter Ward suggests that: 'The Indian seemed a lesser breed of men, given to weakness, servility and, in some cases, villainy.' Talk about giving a dog a bad name...

Asians started coming to Britain in large numbers after the war, which had killed off so many people that Britain was desperate for workers. In 1940, the *Nationality Act* bestowed British citizenship on all colonial and commonwealth citizens, and black people without work in their own lands were encouraged to come to Britain—often to fill the unpopular and dirty jobs, though Asians didn't realise it at the time!

Later, the economic tensions of Asians providing a source of cheap labour riled indigenous communities, who saw this as a threat to their own livelihoods, and this led to racial conflict. By the end of the 1950s, the shortage of labour was less pressing, though the effects of independence continued to drive Asians half way round the world to settle in England's green and pleasant land. But Britain is not the only western country to have received an influx of Asian families.

Indian immigration into Canada started with Sikh soldiers coming from parts of the Far East outside India, and slowly spread to their relations on the sub-continent itself, by the end of the nineteenth century. The first true Asian immigrants arrived in 1906, quite unprepared for the bitterness of the climate—and of the bigots who sought to impose their pre-conditioned stereotypes, seeing us virtually as a threat to public health!

In the first half of the twentieth century, Asians in Canada were tolerated rather than accepted, and it has been largely the political ascendance of India which granted them rights and status in their adopted homeland. As the first president of Ghana quipped: 'Seek ye first the political kingdom and all these things will be added to you.'

In spite of an 'open door' policy towards immigrants right through to the 1970s, fewer Asians sought to live in Canada than in Britain, largely due to fewer jobs being available. A propensity for hard work and an ambition for private enterprise stood in good stead those Asians who have made Canada their home. America has received some 700,000 Asians, while many are still living in African countries. In Jamaica, Asians were expected to give up their own culture and become Jamaican, rather than give their culture to enrich Jamaican society, so tensions have been felt there, too.

A Personal Journey

My own family is typical. I am a Sindhi, a member of a community which has its roots in Hyderabad Sind, now part of Pakistan. We are 'twice-immigrants': in 1946, when the Indian sub-continent was partitioned into the separate countries of India and Pakistan, my Hindu family found itself on the Muslim side of the border, in Pakistan. It was an uncomfortable situation, to say the least. Rather than becoming refugees in India, it seemed sensible to move to a land where we already had business interests.

As Sindhis are renowned for their international trading skills, we had businesses all along the African coast. It seemed natural to leave South Asia, suffering all the pain and conflict of a new born nation in travail. We settled in peaceful Kenya, where I was born in 1950. Little did my family know that we had leapt from the frying pan into the fire, and would soon have to emigrate for a second time.

The trauma of adapting to a new, more western lifestyle was

too much for my father to take. Unable to face the huge responsibilities of a large extended family with impossible expectations, he left my mother a widow at the age of only twenty-two, taking his life by his own hand. (I grew up to regard my uncle as my new 'father', and he is referred to simply as my father elsewhere in this book.)

Though we were a wealthy family in Kenya, with a palatial home and servants, when Kenya gained independence my father was deported and all his family with him. That's actually not too unusual; statistics show that 18% of the Indian population resident in Britain was born in East Africa.

Crestfallen, we wound up in Britain, in the London suburb of Shepherd's Bush. Though Britain had begun restricting the number of immigrants it would accept back in 1962, it was still years away from the legislation which now effectively curtails immigration; so I guess we were lucky to make it into Britain at all. Selling goods was the only thing the Gidoomal family knew how to do, so we all squeezed into four rooms above a newsagents shop.

It was an ignominious start. I remember getting up in what seemed like the middle of the night to deliver newspapers. We did everything ourselves, rather than employ other people; it meant that we could keep what little money we had within our extended family. We'd certainly fallen a long way since the days when we owned a palace, *Moti Mahal*, in Hyderabad Sind.

Like many Asian families, we were business-driven, meeting the needs of the Asian communities around us. We also examined the needs of the British host culture and set out to serve it, making financial killings by opening at times when other traders were still in bed. We stayed open after 9.00pm, to cater for women coming out of Bingo sessions. When we discovered that many of our neighbours were of Irish extraction, we began stocking Irish newspapers and Irish cigarettes.

Becoming a workaholic can place a great strain on family life. Extended family businesses in which all will work together is fine in theory, with a matriarch at home surrounded by daughters and daughters-in-law, and father working with sons at the family business. But the danger is that you lose any sense of your own identity; at what point can you break off to become your own person? Other Asians seem to split their identity, being Asian at home but part of the western host culture once they get outdoors.

Because of the failure to think through issues in a different culture, expectations in the traditional Asian home can become overwhelming. The 'expectation clash' creates a family clash which can break up the home. Elderly folk are often left on their own as the youngsters break off and do their own thing. Many face the dilemma of not wanting to let the family down, yet seeking fulfilment in their choice of career or marriage. The intense pressure this presents in some cases even leads to suicide.

How many people are unaware that they are not alone in these predicaments; that their families are not the only ones going through these traumas—they are being faced in homes nationwide? If the problems besetting western Asians can be faced and resolved, then those who have died tragically need not have died in vain.

'If you can keep your head when all about you
Are losing theirs and blaming it on you...'

CHAPTER

1

BRAVE NEW BEGINNINGS

AS I STOOD ON THE TARMAC at Heathrow airport, in 1967, newly arrived from Kenya, everything seemed strange and unfamiliar.

I'd never seen so many pale faces before, nor witnessed so many odd people in weird clothing. My own outfit felt very strange too; it was the first time in my life that I had ever worn a suit, rather than the shorts and tee-shirt I usually wore in equatorial Kenya. It was a three-piece suit with waistcoat that I'd had made for me in Nairobi, thinking that everyone in Britain dressed like this, and that it would help me to blend in!

There's a story of an English couple who went on holiday to Cairo and found that their European clothing marked them out. After a day of constant harassment from beggars pleading for money, the man bought himself what he took to be an Arab robe similar to the ones all the other men seemed to be wearing. Yet it didn't seem to bring him the dearly wished-for anonymity. On his way out of the hotel the next day, the manager stopped him, pointed at his robe, and politely enquired, 'Excuse me, sir, do you realise that's a lady's nightdress you are wearing?'

That day at Heathrow, I fully expected one of the casually dressed travellers—who'd had the sense to dress for comfort rather than formality—to accost me with similar news. Why did I seem to stand out so much? I later discovered that I had arrived at the very moment that the British fashion scene was being revolutionised by bright, way-out clothing. It was the beginning of the flower power era, and I was dressed like a dull little weed. Few young men of my age wore suits, so I must have looked like a little Lord Fauntleroy. What an embarrassment.

I was blissfully in ignorance of what is called the 'social infrastructure' of the land which I would learn to call my home. Local council offices were geared up to help people like my family and me, but we knew nothing of this till years later. Like many Asian immigrants before and since, my family had already begun to 're-invent the wheel', starting from scratch to discover all we needed to know about the land in which we found ourselves.

Where could we find the rich, spicy food to which we had become accustomed? Where would my mother shop for a sari? How much were these strange English coins worth? Why was the beautiful blue sky I had known all my life suddenly turned an ugly battleship grey? Why was it so cold?

Survival

Fortunately my father, whose calm authoritative presence awaited me after I'd struggled my way through immigration control, had already begun to make some headway in unravelling the mysteries of life in this new land. He had arrived in the UK a year before, staying with relatives until he'd found his feet and bought the shop above which our family was to settle. Together with my brother, sister and a few family members, he was spearheading the trading from a shop which was to become the hub of a business empire. That was the theory, anyway.

We had no information about the grants that might have been available to us, or the kind of help which the state might provide, but asking for charity would have been anathema to us anyway. Instead, we turned to other Asians who had been in Britain for several years; our shop was located in an area where we knew there were other Asian families, to whom we could turn for information or advice.

With the three thousand pounds that we had been able to take out of Kenya, we had bought a home and business—

money went much further in those days! My father had made
friends with other Asians, and it was one of those friends who
had driven him to the airport that day to collect me. Naturally,
the idea of using public transport was not something which we
found attractive. This was an awkward new learning experience
for us. It was not what we were used to, and it would take some
time to grow accustomed to sharing transport with strangers.
Anything which was strange and new filled us with anxiety,
tension, and the fear of looking foolish. Nothing which anyone
else took for granted felt comfortable to us. How on earth were
we going to manage?

Our old mindset gave us no idea of what to expect from life
in Britain, which was exciting but frightening at the same time.
We had 'gone down in the world', and it would take some
getting used to.

Language

Though I had learned to write and speak English in Kenya, and
had even passed my 'O' levels out there, it was very difficult to
get used to the diversity of English accents and the peculiarities
of language with which Londoners peppered their speech.

I was terrified at the way complete strangers called me 'luv'
and 'darlin'. I thought they were making a 'pass' at me! Family
members, who had got used to this English eccentricity,
doubled up with mirth at my embarrassment.

What did they mean when they asked me 'How do you do?'
How do I do *what*?

If someone means 'goodbye', why do they say 'see you
later'?

What does 'Saturday week' mean? It wasn't explained in any
English language book.

Why should people want to 'pull my leg'?

Then there was all that cockney rhyming slang, where someone uses an expression which *rhymes* with the one they intend:
going 'up the apples and pears to Uncle Ned' means going
upstairs to bed, but it doesn't make a lot of sense to the newly-
arrived Asian.

And who were these 'nig-nogs' and 'Pakis' whom some British people seemed to dislike without reason? Why were some of us called 'Gunga Din' when we walked down the street? Didn't people realise that we couldn't 'go back where we came from'? It's a fearful thing to feel unsafe as you sleep in your bed or walk the street in your own neighbourhood.

Though I understood English—often too well for my own peace of mind—my mother had great difficulty with the language, particularly written English. Even now, her writing looks disjointed and crooked, and she finds it embarrassing to write.

Technically, English is difficult to learn because of the large number of irregular verbs. Yet many African languages, Swahili for example, are equally difficult; and there are many different languages within the Asian community. The elderly, though, always seem to find it difficult to get to grips with English; particularly elderly women who lack any regular social intercourse with those outside a tightly-knit Asian community. Often there is no regular contact with native English speakers from whom they can learn the finer points of diction.

I was very embarrassed about my own accent. I felt that I sounded like Peter Sellers lampooning how Asians are supposed to sound! All the time, I feared that people were about to laugh at me because of how I spoke. Yet I quickly acquired a leadership role and, at the tender age of seventeen, I began taking my elders to the local councils and introducing them to the process of enrolling their children in the local schools. That's ironic considering that, even when I knew the answer, I would never put my hand up in the classroom, because I was afraid of my accent being laughed at!

Though my father spoke excellent English, he would often use me to write for him. Spoken English was easier to pick up, because we could watch it being used on the television news; but access to essential resources is usually through paperwork which demands a reasonable command of the written language.

In the 1990s, local authorities frequently produce their paperwork in a range of Asian languages, which makes life easier, but still more needs to be done.

Living Space

When a respectable Asian family arrived in Britain, as so many did during the fifties and sixties, there was never any question of going to the local council for help. That would have been asking for charity, and to use any kind of help other than self-help was to attract stigma.

Friends and relatives who had arrived earlier took it as a matter of pride to offer temporary accommodation to those who had just arrived and who were looking about for a place of their own. Culturally, it is 'not the done thing' to turn away a relative, however difficult it may be to find room for them in a tiny house. Fortunately, it was similarly taboo to stay too long in someone else's home; pride and duty meant that you found a place to live as quickly as possible.

Early immigrants arrived to work in factories in Southall, or on the buses, and then invited village groups to come over and join them. In such ways, a sense of community was maintained, even when transplanted nearly half way across the world. For many East African Asians, it was traditional to be your own boss, and a disgrace to work for someone else. An uncle in Earls Court had given my father a roof over his head and helped him to find a business to buy through *Exchange and Mart*.

Factory jobs can be very menial, but even the most tedious or back-breaking toil was regarded as preferable to the stigma of unemployment. Some uneducated Asians were such good workers that factory bosses encouraged them to have their friends and relatives apply for employment, hoping these would prove to be similarly industrious workers. The extended family was the mechanism by which everyone in the expatriate community earned the opportunity to work and prosper; and the sense of community that this engendered was the primary reward, like a little piece of Asia transplanted to suburban London. Unfortunately, the burning need to create communities sometimes led to the creation of inward-looking ghettos.

The necessity for unfailing good behaviour, regardless of any provocation, has to be drummed into the new arrival; that such provocation will come is a foregone conclusion. Front doors plastered with human excrement and scratches on new paintwork are tame compared with arson attempts. Fortunately the worst days of overt racial attack have now passed.

Some newly-arrived Asians can be alarmed by the western habit of keeping cats and dogs as pets. In hot climates, keeping household pets is considered dangerous; the heat might make them unexpectedly vicious, and in some countries there is a real fear that they could be carrying rabies. In lands which live in constant fear of famine, the idea of feeding unproductive animals is considered irresponsible.

Food

Searching for the right food in an English supermarket makes you realise how a rat must feel in a laboratory maze. Up which gangway must I push my trolley to be rewarded by discovering something edible? Are there any noodles and watercress in this shop? I'm offered some Weetabix instead, but it's not really the same thing, is it? The emotional strain of searching for familiar foodstuffs in a foreign land can be altogether too exhausting.

Asian families are prepared to travel considerable distances to get the kind of food to which they have become accustomed: cumin, coriandar, sesame oil, turmeric, panir (cream cheese), and malai (thick cream). From Shepherd's Bush, my family would strike out before dawn to Covent Garden and Spitalfields markets. It was usually my brother-in-law who went off at 5.00am to buy Indian vegetables and groceries for resale in our local community.

My sister eventually ran one of the very first shops selling Asian food, and she made a small fortune from it. They were able to mark up the food by respectable profit margins.

Of course, that first pioneering generation were usually willing to *try* British food, like pie and chips. But often once was enough; they found it dull and tasteless and they soon went back to traditional spicy Asian food. Meat they would seldom try, if they were used to a vegetarian diet. Oddly, Asian food quickly caught on with the indigenous population, many of whom came to prefer hot spicy curries to their own eel pie mash! Many a successful Asian businessman of today began his business empire serving chicken buna and chapattis to lager-swigging young Englishmen, particularly in cold weather.

If you visit a supermarket in an Asian area today, you will sees shelves sagging under the weight of Indian foodstuffs, which are in tremendous demand. It's not unusual for even the most staid British family to tuck into a curry once a week. But in those far off days, what wouldn't I have given for a constant supply of *Masala Dum Machchi* (spiced baked fish) *Jhinga* (prawns in coconut milk) *Bhuna Murgh* (chicken dry curry) *Badhuk Buffado* (spiced duck) *Akoori* (scrambled egg) *Same Ku Bhaji* (spiced fried beans) *Alu Mattar Sukhe* (potato and pea dry curry) *Nariyal Chatni* (green coconut chutney) *Kela Halwa* (banana sweetmeat) and *Firni* (rice blancmange).

Climate

We nearly froze to death during our first British winter. Our family didn't possess the right clothing to keep us warm, and within a few months we developed back problems and ill health. There was a conflict between wearing the traditional clothing in which we felt comfortable and with which we asserted our Asian identity, and the requirements of the British climate with its freezing winters and howling gales.

It was the first time that we had ever seen snow, apart from on the distant peaks in Kenya. At first the white cotton landscape looked pretty as a picturebook, but soon it had turned to filthy slush. My father slipped on it and hurt his back. He didn't want to waste money buying shoes with non-slip soles, and failed to see that wearing sensible footwear was not simply an aspect of British culture, but a sensible precaution against the treacherous ice. They were not optional extras, but part and parcel of living in Britain.

The climate takes no hostages and eventually we menfolk had to compromise our culture and get some warm overcoats. For the women, it was trickier. Winter coats and saris do not mix and match very well; they don't make an aesthetically pleasing combination. My mother had always worn slippers with her sari and now to replace them with shoes or winter boots was a trial for her and for her sense of identity. Yet without them, she kept slipping and her feet became bitterly cold. Women wearing trousers had been unheard of before and, though some Asian woman resorted to them to keep their legs warm, my own mother wouldn't hear of such a thing. Psychologically, that whole early generation of immigrants found the dull climate profoundly depressing.

We had problems not just with the physical climate. The winds of the cold war were blowing across Europe; the threat of atomic war threatened to plunge the world into a nuclear winter; and Britain was becoming ashamed that it had ever had an empire and didn't much want citizens from the sunnier climes hanging around as reminders.

Distance meant there was little the average Englishman could do about the first two threats, but the third was on his own doorstep or just down the street. The National Front united those who thought people like little Ram Gidoomal and his family were not desired in this green and pleasant land.

Health

Other relatives put up with cold 'for the sake of the children', and were glad to have the National Health Service to take care of their ills and ailments. Goodness, after expensive health care in Kenya it was wonderful to have such excellent medical treatment—and free to boot! I think prescription charges were just coming in at 2/6d (12.5p) but that was nothing compared to the charges to which we had become used. I was pleased with my first free dental checks—till I discovered that I had to have eight fillings.

Like the climate, our health and safety on the physical level was also an apt metaphor for our long-term financial, emotional and spiritual well-being, which depended on the health of the British economy and the goodwill we could generate amongst the dour white faces that passed us in the streets and lanes.

Would Britain come to regard her Asian citizens as malignant tumours and cast us out, as Kenya had done? Foreign exchange regulations had prevented money from being taken out of Kenya during the fraught years leading up to independence—thousands of Asians taking their millions of pounds out of Kenya would have wrecked the Kenyan economy—but my father was eventually allowed back into the country to try to settle his affairs.

When he got back to Mombasa, where the family had lived, he discovered that some of our land had been confiscated, whilst the taxation laws made it difficult to draw together many of the family's other assets. Without an accountant on the spot to bring all the books up to date, much of our wealth was written off. Like other economic exiles, be it the Kurds or refugees from Bosnia, we found that what had once been rightfully ours had now been appropriated by others. My family was partly to blame, of course, because we hadn't taken the trouble to become Kenyan citizens, to build bridges into the African community, or to integrate into the local culture. We had been guilty of reverse-racism, keeping to our safe ghetto.

My father had once feared that he would never be allowed back into Kenya. Now he was there, a greater fear surfaced: perhaps he would not be allowed back into Britain, and might never see his family again...

We had sometimes cowered around the old black-and-white television in our crowded flat and watched the news for the latest utterances from an outspoken government minister, Enoch Powell, who had warned about racial conflict and the 'rivers of blood' which would soon flow. There were terrible people usurping their way into the healthy British heartland, who were ready to overthrow everything the British held dear about their culture. We watched and trembled in disbelief as we came to realise that he was speaking about the black communities, and Asian people like ourselves. We certainly didn't feel like 'the enemy within', some ferocious fifth column conspiring to conquer Britain, as we huddled around our fire trying to keep warm and to drive the flu away through the British winter.

Loss

Pakistan hadn't wanted us because we were Hindus in a Muslim country. We had been rejected by India because we had chosen British citizenship rather than Indian nationality when independence beckoned. Kenya didn't want us because we were not

African. Now Britain didn't seem keen to have us because our skin was a different colour.

On one side there seemed to be posters saying, 'Blacks Go Home!' and on the other side some Asians stupidly protesting with banners proclaiming, 'Disembowel Enoch Powell!'; hardly a good recipe for successful race relations. My own passport called me a 'British protected person': I later discovered that this meant very little. When I started travelling in Europe, I grew accustomed to being turned back at international frontiers because customs officials didn't know what it signified.

'British subjects of the commonwealth and colonies' was another popular designation on passports, and another expression which emphasised inessential differences between the races. Insecurity was the bitter fruit bred of political uncertainties, and it formed a staple diet for Asians struggling with their own identity in a new home.

All this was too much for my father, in 1969. The thought of coming back to the poverty and cold climate of Britain was more than he could stand. He had been in Kenya for several months, like a blackbird with broken wings nursing the ruins of his beloved nest. Father kept extending his trip to delay leaving the relative prosperity of Kenyan life, where many of the family's assets still remained to comfort him. How could he return to his family in a country he could never really learn to like, let alone love?

Running a British newsagent shop depressed him too much. My beloved father took his own life in a way which eye witness accounts record was as undramatic an exit as any suicide can be. This was no cry for help which went wrong, but the final way out for a man under intense pressure. Foul play was not suspected, according to the newspaper cuttings which I keep to this day. I've had two 'dads', and lost them both.

My father was a devout and loving man who single-handedly looked after nearly 100 dependants. He had previously suffered a stroke from the stress and tension of being a twice-migrant, at the age of only 42. Trail-blazing simply took its toll. A devoted father, he ensured that the dowries of each of my unmarried sisters was protected in his will, and that enough was left for my mother's comfort. We boys, of course, were expected to make our own way.

We shed our tears while neighbours packed our little front room to offer their sympathies. They were queueing down the corridor and outside in the street. Though tradition dictated that we close the shop for a three day mourning period, we felt that father would have wanted us to stay open and to continue trading through our grief. In an early break from Asian tradition, this is exactly what we did. Let the women handle the emotion, my brother and I thought; we'll handle the business. We had the fighting spirit in us.

Looking Back

If I could go back in time and meet myself as I was when I stepped off the plane at Heathrow three decades ago, here's the advice I would give myself:

You're part of an Asian family network. Stick in there, because there is safety there; but begin to make inroads, too, into the local British community. Begin to get involved with local issues; begin to befriend English people (and Africans, for that matter) because they are just as human as Asians. Know your own culture, but don't be afraid to make friends outside it. There's a richness to be gained from learning how others see things, and from sharing your own perspective. That would take out one level of the fear that can be so debilitating.

How do you do this? Schools are mono-cultural, but you can make friends with people from other schools, if you're young. Your family might not be too happy, and might try to block your attempts to reach those of other cultures, because there is a long and deep educational process that needs to take place within Asian communities. Educational programmes are needed to break through the barriers and to show diverse cultures meeting and working harmoniously together. Television and newspapers can help in the process, but access to these is beyond the reach of most Asians. The fear of cross-cultural marriages, or marriage to someone of different faith, is hard to conquer.

Advice is plentiful; it's easy to say *what* to do, but *how* to do it is a far more difficult matter. That's something we will address in later chapters...

'If you can trust yourself when all
men doubt you,
But make allowance for their
doubting too...'

CHAPTER

2

A BROWN ENGLISHMAN?

WHEN I FIRST LANDED in Britain, everything had seemed so strange—I might as well have landed on Mars such was the unfamiliarity all around me—but as the days turned into weeks and the weeks into months, I gradually adjusted. In time I came to wonder what all the initial fuss was about. Perhaps this new home wasn't so strange or so bad after all.

How long it took me to acclimatise depends on what you regard as the point at which nothing seems strange any more. If I'm totally honest, there are some things that still hit me as strange even twenty-five years later; but the big initial shock passed after about two years. What helped me as a young person were the last years of my schooling, which served me well as a crash course on all things British or western.

School meals were my first real introduction to western food and, in spite of the jokes that are sometimes made about school dinners, they stood me in good stead in accustoming me to steak and kidney pudding, apple pie and custard. It was very different from the *chapattis*, *ghee* (clarified butter), *curd cheese* and *pulses* to which I had been accustomed. But in a deep sense, though at home in the 1990s I eat western food most of the time, I don't think I've ever really grown to *like* it. I have an Indian friend who doesn't even eat vegetables any more, such are his memories of the stringy cabbage and hard chunks of swede he had to swallow at school lunch time.

A Free Spirit?

The freedom was the first thing which really hit me. Everyone seemed so much freer in the west, not just politically but socially. Without the rigid caste structure that runs like a thread through Indian life, I could mix with different classes of people from social backgrounds I had never previously encountered.

I had freedom now, not simply outside the house, but inside our home, too. In the west, adult males can usually take it for granted that they have immense 'say' in how they run their own lives, without others telling them what to do. They would be surprised—and perhaps shocked—by the great authority which the senior male, the patriarch, has within the average Asian home. He makes decisions on behalf of the whole family, and controls aspects of the lives of the individuals within it which would be unthinkable within a British home.

My father had held such authority in the home as I grew up; but now that he was no longer with us, his role and authority had passed down to his male children. My brothers and I suddenly found ourselves ruling the roost. We were able to make the most of the cultural and social freedoms in British society at large without initially feeling any conflicts from within the home and family life, because there was no longer an authority figure from an older generation to keep check upon us.

What I am about to say may still shock a few Asians, and amuse a few indigenous westerners at my sobriety and naivety. What terrible sins and over-indulgences did I fall into once I was let off the parental rein? Well, actually, I started going down to the local pub—the *General Smuts* opposite my school in Bloemfontein Road, Shepherds Bush—and to acquire a taste for a pint of good hand-pumped bitter!

It was a funny kind of freedom, really. I felt that I could do as I liked, but ended up 'following the crowd' and doing what everybody else did. They went to the pub and drank bitter; so I went to the pub and drank bitter. Some friends started going to body building classes; nine stone weakling that I was, I decided to go to body building classes too. Football? The people round about trooped loyally off to Loftus Road to support Queens Park Rangers for every home game; so I went along and adopted them as my team, too. And on it went, like a madcap game of 'follow the leader'.

Actually, when I tried to take up smoking because everybody else seemed to smoke, I failed miserably. Every cigarette made me ill; but being a non-smoker was about the limit of my individuality.

I'd heard some excellent pop music while I was in Kenya, but being in Britain, I found that I could hear the hits immediately, rather than hearing British hits months late. My siblings were soon spending their pocket money on these records—some of which were starting to employ sitars and other Indian instruments in an exciting and exotic blend of the east and west. When the Beatles started 'going out' with the Maharishi Mahesh Yogi, my Asian friends and I went, 'Hey, these westerners are starting to get into eastern philosophy; we have really got it right!'

Eventually some of us started to go as a family group to the London discotheques that were blossoming in London's West End. Though no one else in my family joined me, I began going to youth clubs, too; it was there that I began to do my body building, and to play table tennis. It seemed a great luxury to have a whole building dedicated to the needs of young people, where they could enjoy and participate in healthy pastimes.

Cultural integration took place at many levels in the youth club—paid for by the local council, too—as it did in many places outside the home. But once we returned to that little flat above the shop, it still felt as though we were crossing an artificial barrier. My siblings and I, though we had been in England only a couple of years, had been born and brought up in a culture outside of India—we were second generation immigrants. But our mother, aunts and uncles had been raised on the Indian sub-continent; they were first generation immigrants—and I gradually came to realise that this meant profound cultural differences in the ways we looked at the world. I looked with western eyes, *but my mother's eyes were eastern.*

Culture Shock!

Often the biggest problem for second generation immigrants is not internal family conflicts—persuading parents of the desirability of taking a full part in British life—but of convincing the indigenous population of the possibility, and of the mutual benefits. Many young Hindus actively *want* their children to belong to Britain, even though their roots just one generation ago were growing in the rich tropical soil of the Indian subcontinent.

In *Citizens of This Country*, their survey of 160 Asian families in Birmingham, Mary Stopes-Roe and Raymond Cochrane write: 'Part of the stability of any social and cultural system resides in the agreement of its members that the system is functional and beneficial.' Only partly in jest, they indict the strong English identity and racial prejudice when they say, 'English people invented the word 'British' in order to be joined with Ireland, Scotland and Wales without sacrificing their Englishness.'

If it's now hard becoming a British citizen, it's even harder being accepted as English with sallow skin the colour of mine; yet it's often not a *conscious* attempt to exclude me. Spending my formative years in Africa meant that I missed out on many of the unifying influences that people my age who lived in Britain through the fifties can remember.

Take children's TV characters for example: I knew about Bill and Ben the flower pot men, but who was Muffin the Mule and Andy Pandy? What was it like living here in the grim post war years, when the country was getting back on its feet? What was this 'smog' that Londoners my age remember from their childhood? Why do people still hate the Moors Murderers? There will always be parts of recent British history which I can read about, but to which I will forever be a stranger because I didn't live through them.

It's wrong even to think simply of 'British' culture and 'Indian' culture. Culture—by which we mean *acquired and disciplined patterns of responses of an individual or society to various internal and external stimuli*—is forever changing and evolving, never standing still long enough for anyone to hang a sign on it except retrospectively. British youth culture changed drastically in the 1950s, and not simply because that is when immigrants began to arrive in large numbers.

Changes had already begun to happen because of the post-war baby boom, which had created the 'teenager' as a distinct cultural entity. Before, boys gradually became men, and girls women; now there was a semi-unified 'young people' with aspirations different from children and adults alike. By the 1960s, this group was numerically large and economically active; Britain was in flux.

Older people possibly placed blame upon immigrants which might rightly have been placed on the shoulders of indigenous white young people. A whole generation rejected many of the values of its forebears; a people in motion. Older people were frightened of this and, in their fear, lashed out at anything and everything which seemingly smacked of change. Asians caught some of the backlash of reaction to cultural changes they had played no part in bringing about.

Perhaps these are the true roots of modern racism.

Identity Crisis

Within the four walls of home, many second generation immigrants find themselves in 'Little India' or 'Little Asia'. In the outside world they are gaining new experiences and discovering new ideas; but when they return home, they have to pack up these experiences and ideas and put them away out of sight. They are not wanted out 'on show' in the traditional Asian home.

When I used to go to the pub and return with my clothing smelling of smoke, I had to go upstairs and quickly change because I knew that my elders didn't like it. These little deceptions are not uncommon in many Asian homes; though I'm informed that it's not an exclusively immigrant phenomenon. Many ordinary young people from white middle-class backgrounds keep such secrets from their parents as well!

Because in a normal Asian family there is a level of trust, these deceptions can prey heavily on the minds of the perpetrators. I was not the only member of my family living a 'double life'; when the pressures and tensions of a dual existence grew too much for one extended family member, he tried to take his own life and ended up in hospital having his stomach pumped out. The settling-in process, and a sense of loss, had proved overwhelming for him.

Young people's feelings of not belonging are aggravated by other pressures of life, such as failing examinations, sexual harassment at work, or developing relationships which are frowned on as inappropriate by the family head.

A survey of Asian youth in Newcastle upon Tyne as far back as 1976 clearly laid the main grounds of conflict and split them into various categories: Religion, friendship, marriage, education and employment. (We will be looking at these issues in further chapters.) It was more than twenty years since the exodus to Britain had got under way—plenty of time for a second generation of Asian immigrants to fully feel the alienation and sense of 'not belonging' which has since grown to epidemic proportions. They clearly expressed this feeling of being 'outsiders', and their crisis of identity.

About a third of those interviewed said that they wanted to return to India (a land many of them had never even seen), a third wished to remain in Britain, and a third just didn't know. Reasons given in the survey (published as *The Half-Way Generation*) for staying included:

Better living standard here.
This is my home.
I like the people/country/weather.
My family is over here.

Reasons for returning included:

It's my country and it needs me.
There is more freedom.
There are relations there.
I can make more money there.
I won't stand out as coloured.

'I don't think I could ever be English', said one of the respondents; 'Anything I do, I've got to be careful,' cautioned a second. 'I don't mind if they leave you alone, but they don't,' another lamented. This is typical of most of the surveys that have been conducted into Asian cultural adaptation.

Worlds in Collision

If young Asians are worried about the problems of how to fit into the society in which they find themselves, then older people are concerned at whether such a 'fitting-in' is even desirable. Perhaps the compromises will prove to be too great. They are anxious about what they see as the rejection of Asian traditional values by these 'children of the exodus'—the second generation immigrants.

In the 1990s, in Wembley, Alperton or Southall— those parts of West London where there are sizeable Asian communities I see more and more Indians reverting to Asian clothing. I usually wear a suit or casual western clothing myself; I take a delight in wearing traditional Indian clothing when the social context justifies it, though I used to be untypical in this. Now there seems to be a backlash from older Asians against western culture.

Sociologically speaking, feelings of transience, traumatically coupled with bad experiences of British society and life style, led many first generation migrants to reject British culture as a viable or desirable alternative to their own. Contacts with the local population were minimised, and continuing relationships with Asians (in Asia or Britain) has been put at a premium. A separate or self-contained satellite of Asian culture has developed.

The survey published in *Citizens of this Country*, indicated that 82% of mothers (but only 15% of daughters) wore traditional Indian clothing 'as often as possible', suggesting a very strong desire on the part of the older generation to retain the old culture. Fathers were far less keen on this aspect of Asian culture, only 11% choosing to wear Indian garb as often as feasible. A rapid falling away of the desire to retain traditional dress was indicated by the fact that only 3% of sons expressed an enthusiasm for frequent wearing of Indian clothing—90% of sons begrudgingly wearing traditional dress only 'when obliged to'.

Rather than seeking to 'fit in' with traditional British life, many older Asians still strive to transplant their own culture into the west. Certainly Asians in Britain are now starting to form their own clubs, such as *The Patel Club* for Asian businessmen, possibly because they have been refused membership of white clubs, but equally probably because they want to run such establishments on more traditional lines.

New Asian newspapers seem to spring up with alarming regularity, to provide a sense of Asian identity not present in white-run periodicals, but often mirroring the insular problems of never looking beyond one's own immediate situation and cultural cirmumstances.

Asian shops, videos, satellite television, bhangra music, dance raves and radio stations are all symptomatic of the desire to resist complete integration into British culture. Often these 'Asian equivalents' are not completely Asian but reflect a true fusion of two cultures, a new 'British Asian' culture. In other countries, we will see the arrival of the Canadian Asian, the Caribbean Asian, the South African Asian, and so on.

It's important to understand that this culture is being created by two different kinds of immigrants—the willing and the reluctant, but mainly the former; in fact, the reluctant can usually be classed as forced immigrants or refugees.

Refugees

For many of us Asians who arrived in Britain from East Africa, there is no way back. Neither Africa nor India can be called home any longer; as British subjects with no claims on Kenyan *or* Indian nationality, we are here for good—or for bad.

East African Asians, says Robinson, 'have less restricted aspirations, a built-in drive to social and economic mobility, and a more limited desire to retain community associations... East African Asians seem set on a route which may well end in increased inter-ethnic conflict and group marginalisation.'

That's exactly what happened in Kenya in my experience,

and I hear that it happened too in other East African countries. Asians were so 'pushy', aggressive and successful that the local community couldn't keep up, were left out, and felt threatened by Asians visibly making so much money and spending it conspicuously on big houses and servants. It was done in an insensitive and opulent way that created the antagonism which—I believe—ultimately led to Asians being expelled.

When we came to Britain, we began to make the same mistakes all over again! My family bought a colour television at the time when they were still something special, and a brand new Rover car—which got scratched, probably in a moment of antagonism and jealousy because we were doing so well, prospering and expanding from one shop to a string of nearly half a dozen. 'If you've got it, flaunt it,' is a very bad recipe for racial harmony. East African Asians can be very tactless in their drive towards future prosperity.

Though my own family underwent enormous tribulation in being cast out of Kenya, a few years after we arrived other Asian immigrants came in even greater plight. I mean, of course, the Asians who were deported from Uganda by Idi Amin in 1973.

These were refugees in every sense of the word. Forced to leave behind virtually all their wealth when they were airlifted from Entebbe Airport, many arrived in Britain with little beyond the clothing they stood up in. 28,000 Ugandan Asians had arrived in Britain by April 1973, to the embarrassment of the government, who housed them in sixteen disused army camps prepared as reception centres. Research conducted a year later showed that 45% of heads of families were still out of work, many of them living on a minimum of state benefit. *69% of all adults could not speak English.* Many of them, particularly the elderly, were terribly lonely. Most felt completely at a loss. Formerly well-to-do people, in Britain they felt like second class citizens.

Journalist Brenda Kidman (in her book *A Handful of Tears*) eloquently evokes the next stage for some Asians who were found move-on accommodation in a Tunbridge Wells house furnished by local welfare organisations: 'Mammoth mahogany wardrobes with freckled mirrors appeared in the bedrooms, along with tallboys smelling of camphor, and high bedsteads clamped between headboards as forbidding as a medieval portcullis. Ruptured armchairs and sofas trussed up in faded chintz graced the ground floor lounge, and there was a bamboo occasional table which sagged precariously beneath a pile of outdated *Country Life* magazines.

'Most of the floorboards had at least one square of threadbare Axminster and if the curtains on the huge sash windows didn't quite reach the sills, someone unpicked the hems and let down the frayed edges until they did.' It's all a far cry from the tropical breezes and the exotic sounds of Africa to which they must surely have grown accustomed.

Harassment ranged from lighted newspapers pushed through letter boxes, to a sudden rash of 'Asians Go Home' posters—a futile move when people no longer have a home to which they can return. Would Queen Victoria have been amused to spot the dishevelled remnants of her Indian Empire trying to scratch a living by flogging curry and chips...

By April 1975, a follow-up survey of 130 particularly needy families revealed scores still on state benefit—a great indignity to those who had been accustomed to making their own way in Uganda. Many families had one or more old, sick or handicapped relatives to look after, who felt bewildered and lost in a vast friendless city. Large one-parent families were approaching a crisis point, as infants screamed themselves to sleep at night, and widows were left to fend for themselves. What a disgrace!

The Myth of Return

For those Asians who came to Britain of their own will, directly from the Indian sub-continent, the perspective is a little different. Many harbour aspirations of making their fortunes in Britain and then returning there, though it's unlikely that this will ever happen. Towns like Dayalpur, in the Punjab, are rapidly becoming ghost towns because so many have moved to Britain, and so few returned!

The once-migrant came to Britain to send money back home and improve the social standing of his family in India.

Dayalpur's bizarre local economy, for example, has led to the construction of a sophisticated new hospital and telephone exchange serving an illiterate population of 900 people—all of whom seem regularly to make grateful phone calls to their relatives in Britain! As economic migrants, these relatives regard themselves as sojourners or temporary Britons.

Asians who have arrived via East Africa tend to have no aspirations to send money back to India, where contact with relatives is less frequent. Twice-migrants are usually more stable and settled in Britain.

Conversely, Asians who migrated directly from the sub-continent decades ago seem stuck in a time warp and often carry with them an Asian cultural identity based on what they remember from the 1960s, 50s or even 40s. They haven't had the intervening years in India, so their attitudes and sense of India's morality has not moved with the times; even their use of Indian languages has frozen in time. When they do go back to India they get a double culture shock because India has moved on from where they left it, and is no longer how they remember it. They are shocked to find discos in Karachi and Calcutta, though they are now quite common.

They find that 'queue jumping' is not a uniquely western trait—it happens in India too—and bribing officials is far more common. It's easier to get justice in Britain than in South Asia. The wealthy in Bombay are as guilty of conspicuous consumption as any British millionaire in Hampstead or Windsor. The rich in Delhi are like characters from an American soap opera, with their gold-embossed calling cards; and don't mention the appalling driving of Indian motorists!

Whilst frowning at the permissive society of Britain in the 80s and 90s, and contrasting it unfavourably with the India they remember, they fail to realise that Indian society has gone through many of the same changes, often at the same time, and is in many places as permissive as the west.

Clandestine night clubs have sprung up in India's urban sprawls, in which Asian girls dance for Asian men in a way the clients would never allow their own daughters to do. Prostitution and drug abuse are rampant on the streets of Delhi and

Bombay in a way they never were in those cherished sepia-toned memories of India. The rich have got richer and the poor have got poorer. Asians in Britain are often pining for a land which no longer exists, if it ever did. They might as well pine for Atlantis or Never-Neverland.

Zerbanoo Gifford (in her book *The Golden Thread: Asian Experiences of Post-Raj Britain*) expresses the situation beautifully: 'When Asians first travelled to Britain they held onto their suitcases, collecting souvenirs to take home with them and thereby created the myth of return. Now the second generation, born in Britain, is clearly here to stay and it is up to them to claim their just place and voice within British society...

'Our children are the golden thread which ties us to the future; through their lives we are kept alive and can continue to grow... The thread between two cultures which is being woven by the new generation should not be broken by the fear of cultural contamination. Certain change is inevitable within any society, but we can feel sure that Indian culture which has developed over thousands of years will not disappear overnight.'

Even first generation once-migrants—those still most firmly attached to the Indian homeland—must eventually come to accept that the west is now their terminus, not their waiting room.

A Middle Ground

To summarise: The refugee status felt by many twice-migrants, and the 'myth of return' amongst South Asians has delayed complete wholesale assimilation into British culture. Some Asians have completely retained their Asian culture; some have abandoned it altogether and have embraced western values like long-lost friends; but most are still feeling the strains and pressures of being 'the piggy in the middle'.

K.T. Kannan's research in the Southall Asian community in 1978 (self-published as *Cultural Adaptation of Asian Immigrants*) predicts that where there is stiff rejection from the host society in accepting the new generation of immigrant groups, many will quickly swing back to their Indian cultural roots.

Others will regard themselves as English, regardless of the level of acceptance, or lack of it. A third alternative is to remain somewhere between two cultures, and become a cultural amalgam rather like European Jews or the Parsees in India.

'Full assimilation cannot be acheived as long as the resistance from the other side is continued,' Kannan concludes. 'Large scale inter-marriages, colour change and the consequent relatively easy assimilation, cannot be realised in the near future. In the coming few generations, the inter-generational conflict in the family, the rejections of the host society and the feelings of frustration and other problems would possibly result in a 'cultureless' society... They may have certain vague elements or traits from the Asian culture still lingering, but the major elements will be from the receiving society...

'On the whole, it may not be unreasonable to conclude that (1) there will be organised religious and cultural groupings of Asians extending over a few generations in the future; (2) there will also exist side-by-side another group of 'cultureless' or 'floating' individuals, and (3) drawing members from these three groups, the strength of the inter-racially married individuals would gradually increase, and this group can have no other aim than complete assimilation into the host society.'

I think we will also see the ascendance of the 'Western Asian', the creator of a new society which merges the best of two cultures. There is, of course, a danger that we will end up merging the *worst* aspects of two cultures, the narrow-minded and petty bigotry...

We live in an age of great change—and great consequence.

'If you can wait and not be tired by waiting,
Or being lied about don't deal in lies...'

CHAPTER

3

A TIME FOR LEARNING

I N ASIAN CULTURE, it is important to have a good education in order to get a good job, so as not to burden your family. 'Get on in life' is probably the golden rule in many Asian households.

Myself, I studied hard to pass my 'O' and 'A' levels, to win a place at Imperial College to study Physics, where I eventually studied for my doctorate. On my long and rambling way through the educational process, I also acquired substantial business skills from my relatives, so education was not simply classroom-based. Living in Kenya, I had to learn Swahili to communicate with the Africans who worked for the family. This was in addition to Sindhi to speak with family members; Hindi to understand Asian films and plays; and English for my school-work. Most of my school friends spoke Gujarati and Kutchi, so I picked up these languages, too. All of them have since served me well in the world of commerce.

My own children don't have the range of languages which I have acquired; they don't speak Hindi, Gujarati and Sindhi— or Swahili for that matter. This doesn't worry me unduly because we are in Britain to stay, and those languages are not essential to their education. Neither do they dress in Asian clothing, though they might in future, when they find their Asian roots. These third generation immigrants don't like their food so hot, so the family's diet is mainly western, with Asian food prepared only one day per week. In my youth, I was encouraged to play the harmonium, the sitar or the tabla—but my children play cello, clarinet or piano. It's all part and parcel of being educated in Britain.

In Kenya, only poor families went in for scholarships because rich families could afford to pay the full fees, and took it as a matter of pride to do so. In Britain, where education comes free, scholarships take on a different meaning; they are a symbol of prestige, and a sign of academic achievements. Times are changing.

I was brought up as a Hindu, though there was a strong Sikh influence, too; but I am now a follower of Christ. I have seen no evidence in Britain of Asian children being encouraged to take seriously the religious aspects of traditional Hinduism as part of their informal education, though many are being attracted to the so-called 'new gurus' such as Sai Baba and Muktananda. They are finding meaning and expression there, and it is acceptable to even the most conservative and traditional Asian parents, in spite of the conflicts between traditional Hindu thought and the teachings of modern day gurus.

I find that racial harassment is something I still take steps to avoid wherever possible. Even when driving there are certain 'No Go areas', like Tower Hamlets, which I try to avoid going through if at all feasible. This is something which I try to pass on to my children, though I yearn for the time when it becomes unnecessary. It doesn't make me feel insecure, and I'm happy in my neighbourhood in Sutton, Surrey. Yet even here, if my son is coming home by public transport after dark, I'm inclined to collect him at the station.

My hope is that my children will work hard at school, sit their examinations, do well, go to college, get good jobs, and excel. I want them to adapt well to life in England—unlike many first generation immigrants who don't want to see any changes, and sometimes even send their children to school in India!

Academically, the concept of Asian immigrants experiencing 'psychological tension as a result of the clash between their domestic cultural tradition and those of society at large' is a theme recurring through all the educational studies and surveys conducted in the field. Eventually, the children caught between Indian and British culture will resolve their conflicts. The question is, what type of schooling will best help them towards that objective? Should it be a mainly Asian school, or mainly white? There are pros and cons to each view.

Schools

It's easy to say that schools that are 90% non-white will inhibit cross-cultural growth and encourage a ghetto mentality, but— on the positive side—it can generate a 'warmth of numbers' and give *some* bewildered immigrant children a sense of security. It can provide a focus for the cultural and social life of an ethnic community. In educational terms, resources for the teaching of other cultures, or special English classes for those not fluent in the language, can be concentrated efficiently in particular schools.

Negatively, it can reduce contact between the immigrant and the white community, prevent social and economic mobility, and lead to general polarisation, say the experts. Educational apartheid can develop, preventing the cross-fertilisation of cultures, producing a short-sighted view of the wider world. There is a danger of encouraging stereotyped views if there is inadequate mingling of ideas and experiences.

Culturally-integrated schools can help to break down prejudice. People of different cultures who have been to school together get on better than if they have been artificially segregated till adulthood. My niece, Sheena, experienced this during her time in the cosmopolitan hotbed of Cheltenham Ladies' College. There is greater possibility for creative exchanges in a classroom where Asian Britons and white Britons can discuss together subjects like *'British colonialism in nineteenth century India'*. Such discussions may prevent the next generation from repeating the mistakes of the past. Syllabus changes which enable Asian literature, music and drama to be studied would help with integration, but—perhaps most important—is the need for history to be taught from viewpoints other than that of the British Empire! It is good to draw on the perspectives of other cultures.

In practice, the major problem is that we Asians often tend to gather in communities rather than being dispersed throughout a town or city. Local schools in urban areas can become severely over-subscribed with Asian pupils, leading to all-black schools, regardless of the educational pros and cons. Bangladeshis seem particularly disadvantaged in this regard. Dispersal, by bussing children to schools further afield, can have educational advantages, but can also be traumatic for pupils separated from their friends and siblings. Parents are denied choice of school for their children, who may then make poor educational progress because of their limited command of English in a school where there is no provision for special English classes.

There can be further difficulties when teachers are all white, and do not live in the area where they teach. Cultural imperialism is inherent in the British educational system, and it won't go away overnight. There are no easy solutions.

Schooling

A 1980 report by the *Catholic Commission for Racial Justice* concluded that learning problems experienced by some Asian children stem both from the urban poverty in which many of them live, and from their particular position between two cultures.

There is evidence that bi-lingual children should be given an opportunity to become proficient in their mother tongue. A better grasp will increase their ability to learn, comprehend and express themselves in English, because they will be less likely to confuse the two languages.

Some speak dialect English and become confused and disenchanted to discover that the English they have learned is not 'proper' English. The report said: 'Not only can black pupils feel rejected by society's rejection of the linguistic forms in which they express themselves, but black pupils will sometimes use dialect as a base for a separate identity and as a way of rebelling against the school, authority or society generally.

'Schools must understand the complexities of language that black children have to deal with, and their various forms of language should be respected and as far as possible incorporated into the life of the classroom.' This should create a more amenable context in which to explain and teach the 'standard' English without which communication and performance in other subjects will be impaired.

In assessment, the report found that many of the standard tests are 'culturally loaded' against immigrants, not simply because of language difficulties, but also because of lack of familiarity with the subject matter and the form of testing. A bright pupil can actually come across as dim-witted, when their highly-developed reasoning skills are concealed by lack of culturally-determined 'information' with which to utilise those skills. Poor assessment performance can then affect the self-esteem of bright pupils.

The development of a sense of identity is important if education is to produce complete and fully-rounded people, rather than emotionally-retarded adults who have been stuffed with information like battery hens.

An Asian child from a distinct alternative culture has a clear cultural identity upon which to fall back. But if the alternative culture has become partly westernised, then mixed culture can present a child with indistinct cultural roots. The child is often not able to find his or her own identity between two cultures because it has become impossible to grasp the essence of each culture when neither culture is clearly distinguishable. It can be like trying to play football without knowing which team you are on, or where the goalposts are!

'If a school is to be supportive of black children in their search for a sense of identity and self-esteem, the ethos and curriculum of the school must provide a multi-cultural experience supplying children with significant black heroes from their culture of origin, and teachers must understand how dialect, street culture and rebellion may be part of a search for identity and self-esteem.

'It is particularly important that black children are able to develop strong personal relationships with black adults whom they can look up to, and in this respect the shortage of black teachers in our schools is an urgent problem,' says the report.

Communication between home and school is not always the best it could be, either.

Young People

Many Asians are terrified of the lack of discipline which exists, in their eyes, in the local white community. This is a big factor in their first choice of where to send their children. If they can afford it, Asians will go for private schooling. Statistically, a larger proportion of Asians send their children to private schools than the population as a whole. We believe that our children will get a better education, become more disciplined, and—when they become young people—have a better chance of landing a good job, and benefit from greater job security through this route.

Being part of the family business is one thing, but even we Sindhis like our children to have an independent professional qualification. If there is an Asian and a white person going for the same job, with equal qualifications, I know who will be offered the job! Only by having better qualifications can the Asian candidates compete equally.

Muslims are very keen to have their own schools, though I have not detected Hindus with the same desire for specifically Hindu schools. It's a religious matter, but one related more to 'matters of practice' than to belief; Muslims like their own schools because they don't like Muslim girls doing P.E. with the boys. Strict Muslim laws tend to militate against Muslim pupils fitting in to most British state schools, which they see as being run on Christian principles—though most of them are not. Hindus are open to everything—except perhaps to militant Islam! Sufism seems more acceptable to many Hindus than does orthodox Islam.

It's generally accepted now that education is not something limited exclusively to the classroom, but little informal *religious* learning takes place in the Asian home. Hindu girls may be expected to join their parents at the temple as they reach their teens, but boys have greater freedom to do as they please. Boys are expected to be out making money in business, so they are excused these mundane religious duties. Unlike in Christianity, personal faith is low down on the agenda; *the family has a faith which it follows, and individuals within the family follow it because they are family members. A strong emphasis is placed on observing religious rituals. This is regarded as being more important than the underlying faith.*

Surveys show that Asians in the west, young and old alike, would like to make more visits to the Indian sub-continent. Nearly two-thirds of second generation young people had not been to their parents' country in the previous ten years (according to Stopes-Roe and Cochrane's survey, published in 1991) while only 17.5% of first generation immigrants had not been back in all that time. Clearly the desire to look at the old country quickly diminishes with each generation.

93% of first generation immigrants said they remained in contact with a family 'back home'. For the second generation, only 26% maintained a direct contact (i.e. communicating themselves with someone in India) though two-thirds maintained contacts through other family members.

By every measurable criteria, second generation Asian young people are more distant from their country of origin than are their parents.

Youth and the Media

The media often provide young Asians with important role models. The Chinese have old Bruce Lee films to give them an idealised impression of how young Chinese people might behave, and South Asians have role models too, in the Indian film industry.

Amitabh Bachchan is the most popular Asian film star of the early 1990s. His brother owns *TV Asia*, on the Astra satellite. A more localised role model is Danny Charanji, a Birmingham DJ who is very popular and idolised by young people. A flashy superstar who plays Bhangra music and produces his own recordings, Danny has the status symbol of owning a Birmingham penthouse.

Much learning takes place informally, through reading magazines, watching television, or viewing films on video. Though these are useful sources of information, they are also a way of subconsciously picking up prejudices and attitudes which really need to be countered. Much of what we watch on our television screens has originated in the United States, and research into American cinema shows some disturbing trends.

In a well-researched dissertation, Eugene Wong has shown that 'The portrayal of Asians in American feature films reflects and influences white Americans' perception of Asians and Asian Americans... A considerable part of white America's non-cinematic relations with Asians has been the product of racism, myth and assumption.' Films typically portray abnormal and unequal racial relations between Asians and whites.

This must clearly lead to non-Asians forming wrong ideas about Asians—though it's unlikely to impact on the self esteem of first generation immigrants who seldom watch English films or television programmes. When we first came to Britain, my parents watched only one programme, an Asian affairs slot which used to go out on a Sunday morning. My siblings and I would tune to the news, *Top of the Pops*, soap operas, and a whole range of viewing.

Statistics have shown that Asian young people watch TV much more than their elders, and two-thirds read English newspapers regularly, exposing themselves far more than their parents to views and attitudes very different to those with which they have been brought up—a factor likely to exaggerate cultural differences.

Most parents said they didn't read English papers at all. Almost all Asian mothers revealed that they had never read English papers; 90% of them (and 44% of Asian fathers) reported that their ability to *read* English was non-existent. In a survey of 120 British Asian young people, none described their own ability to read English as non-existent; and most described their English reading as 'good'.

The use and relative proficiency of languages in an Asian household can be totally bewildering. 'The language I use most after English is Gujarati, but I cannot read or write it,' explained one British-born Asian. 'I can understand Urdu well enough although it is difficult to speak, but I can read and write it. The reason for this is that Urdu is regarded by my parents as a high-class language which a person must learn in order to achieve a high status in the community, and my parents placed a lot of emphasis on me learning the language. They were not really concerned that I could not read or write Gujarati even though they mentioned a few times that I should learn it. They were much more concerned that my written English should improve.' (Cited by Harris and Savitzky in *My Personal Language History*.)

Language

Learning English is probably the one area of adult education which many first generation immigrants (particularly one-time immigrants who have come straight from India) will certainly find indispensible.

A typical English course for adults will begin with basic meeting, greeting and leaving phrases: Hello, how are you today? Goodbye now. Learning English numbers, and simple requests and instructions might follow. They will be taught how to make a polite request, then how to be more insistent without becoming rude. They may learn how to apologise, and how to correct someone else's mistake politely, and what to do and say when they are not understood. This can all be a great boost to self-confidence.

Later, a typical English course might teach how to express likes and dislikes; expressing preferences; how to shop; understanding bus timetables; and giving and receiving simple directions: 'Where is the post office, please?'

It is particularly important that every Asian is able to shop without being exploited, and without giving offence to the shopkeeper. When buying a jacket, for example, it may be necessary to specify a colour; politely reject an offered item; redefine the colour; give an indication of style; and indicate the price range within which they are looking. In the last resort, the customer needs to know how to get out of the shop without feeling obliged to purchase something they don't want. It helps to know simple phrases like, 'Oh, I'm afraid that's too expensive. I think I'll have to leave it then. Goodbye.'

It's all very obvious once you've tenaciously acquired the

vocabulary; but until that time, shopping can be a nightmare. Imagine trying to purchase a pair of shoes and not knowing how to say, 'I'm afraid this shoe doesn't fit,' or 'Have you got any lace-ups?'

These are just the essentials of spoken English needed to get by, and written English is a whole different ball game.

Children and Language

Sue Barley teaches language skills to immigrant children in the deprived London borough of Newham, where almost half the population is Asian. 'We work by supporting subject teachers, and not by withdrawing children from classes for language tuition, because that would separate and stigmatise those with poor language skills.'

Financed by the Home Office rather than an education authority, Sue recently supported a P.E. teacher by organising a treasure trail around nearby Wanstead Flats. Linguistic clues made the developing of essential language abilities into an interesting pastime, instead of a chore to be slaved over.

The teachers with whom she works have to pledge themselves to spend at least a half hour for each lesson, planning the use of materials which will convey language skills—tricky in subjects other than English language. It works by carefully putting pupils into groups of about six, typically with two or three with poor language skills and the rest with good skills. These groups are not selected along friendship lines. The pupils can learn as much from one another as they do from the teacher.

'For GCSE English, they are studying J.B. Priestley's play *An Inspector Calls*, which takes place mainly in one room. It's incredibly difficult for a pupil with low English ability to understand, so there I help the immigrant and refugee pupils to 'access the curriculum', by discussing and working on it together. We're not allowed to just give them something easier to do, we have to help them to understand this difficult play.

'Part of my job is to raise teachers' awareness of the problems of immigrants. Some teachers are shocked by the idea of switching pupils from sitting in rows facing the blackboard, to sitting together in little groups discussing the subject with each other.'

The group method sometimes causes problems for pupils who have studied overseas in a much more disciplined way. It takes some time for them to appreciate the advantages of being able to pick up a good command of English from other pupils.

Poor command of language is not simply a problem in itself, it exacerbates every other problem where communication is important. It runs as a theme through the whole of life, much as it recurs as a motif throughout this book!

Higher Education

When my own turn came for higher education, I didn't automatically qualify for a grant, as I'd only been in Britain for 18 months. Fortunately, because of my good GCE results, the local authority waived the rules which said that I should have been in the country for three years to qualify. When the 1970s arrived, local authorities were hardly ever so understanding or as generous to Asian would-be students again.

Local authority grants usually require that a student's parents make a sizeable contribution; but since my natural father and the uncle I had come to call my father were both deceased, the family's funds were still frozen in Kenya, and fifteen people were living off one shop, the authority sensibly set the parental contribution at zero.

I was a student at Imperial College at the same time as some other students who later became world famous as members of the rock band *Queen*, though I never knew them. Loneliness and isolation became my chief companions during the time the college required me to live in a hall of residence for a period. All by myself, it was a miserable experience. I had to do my own shopping, wash my own clothing, make the effort to build relationships and construct a life for myself.

My friend and colleague Dr Raju Abraham has written that 'loneliness can be defined as the loss of intimacy or closeness. You feel left out, cut off and alienated from those around you. A change of job or house, moving to a new culture or the death of someone close to you, can all contribute to feeling lonely.' I qualified in all those regards!

College social clubs and activities like the Sailing Club provided me with new contacts, but friendships were hard to cement; I'd never done it before, and I just didn't know where to begin. Everyone seemed to be on a different wavelength, with a different perspective to life than myself. People would say things and I would constantly think 'but I don't agree with that'. As an Asian, I found I had a very different way of looking at everything, but I didn't dare say so!

I soon learned that pubs were the places where many people went at that time. If you bought a pint and sat there for long enough, people would chat to you. After a few beers, I felt less embarrassed about my Asian accent; the alcohol gave me the illusion of greater confidence, and I wasn't afraid to speak to people any longer. It was trivial conversation though; I couldn't talk about the matters which were really important to me.

There were pressures on me to submit to an arranged marriage; but if I spoke about it to the average Englishman, he would probably have thought the whole idea was hugely funny. He simply wouldn't be able to grasp the problem; he'd just have a great laugh at my expense. Often, I'd stay in my room reading and working just to keep busy; anything to fill the empty hours and days.

I wouldn't even go to the lounge to watch television because there would be so many people there whom I didn't know. The environment felt so alien, so different, so hostile. London is worse than many other places; in Britain's capital, people typically don't even know their next door neighbours, whereas in other parts of the country there is more social interaction on a community basis. In London, no one seems to ever speak to anyone they don't already know. After three months, I couldn't take it any longer. I packed up my belongings and moved out of the hall of residence back to the tiny home my family shared above our Shepherd's Bush shop.

Lack of information was a problem for me, as it has been for many other Asians in the same situation. There were probably many other people on my course who felt the same way; who were well acquainted with the same loneliness, and made friends with the same fears. One young man was a Roman Catholic, and some nuns came to help him, introducing him to the friendship and fellowship of a local church. For me, there was a distance, a cultural gulf, and I found it impossible to touch another's soul. The isolation in which I found myself was too great, too debilitating. My world was cold and dark.

A Different Education

Yet, in that lonely period away from home, one event occurred which totally transformed my life.

I have always been interested in learning about religions; so much so that my father bought me the Hindu scriptures to read. I was always looking for meaning behind life: why do we exist? At the age of twelve, I was taught that Christianity was always associated with colonialism, so I had a negative attitude to it that had remained unchanged by coming to Britain. But sitting in a pub one day, a group of Christian rock musicians came in, and everyone turned their chairs round to listen. One tune *He's Got the Whole World in his Hands* really struck a chord with me, and some of the texts they quoted seemed familiar.

Then I remembered that my family had once all been given little booklets called *Daily Strength* published by Scripture Gift Mission. Without realising that these were daily readings from the Christian scriptures, *The Holy Bible*, I'd read it several times from cover to cover and been so enthralled that I'd come to know large chunks by rote.

I thought that I might enjoy discussions with these Christian musicians, so I invited them to come to my room, and we had a long discussion. I took the Bible they offered me and read it from cover to cover, but after several weeks of arguments, they concluded I was not interested in getting nearer to God and stopped coming.

I continued to read the Bible on my own, struggling for six months. I read the words of Jesus where he explains that the direct and only route to God *is through himself*—'I am the way and the truth and the life. No one comes to the Father except through me' (John's Gospel 14:6)—but I declined to give my life over to the Lord Jesus Christ. If I did, I thought it would be an acknowledgement that I'd really failed!

In my own strength, in the religions of which I was aware, there was no way out of the trap of sin, or *karma*. There was the concept of repentance in Hinduism, but no way out of the consequences. I could do good, but the bad deeds would still count against me. I believed that I would have to live millions of lives before finally achieving liberation—but there was no indication of how all these lives could possibly make any difference. Simply putting the problem off for millions of years was not going to resolve the problem one iota.

I'd worked out that I was spiritually bankrupt, but when the promise of Christ came along, I thought 'That's interesting. All my sins get wiped out in one stroke; Christ becomes the sin-bearer who takes them all off me.' But could it be true? Coming from a trading family, I had to look for a catch, but I couldn't find one!

I researched the background and discovered that Jesus was someone who had really existed. Unlike most of the figures in Hindu scriptures, he was rooted in history; and unlike the Hindu scriptures, the Bible seemed relevant to modern life in Britain. I said 'Yes, I can give this a shot, I'll invite Jesus into my life and see what difference it makes'.

I had long stood at the crossroads where so many of my relations had stood. My natural father and the uncle whom I'd called my father had stood at this point where life no longer made enough sense for them to go on living. Both seeking their way out of a dilemma, each had taken his own life, expecting to be reincarnated—to be born again—when they really needed to be born again of the Spirit of Christ.

An aunt in East Africa had overdosed, and a family member in London had unsuccessfully tried to blot out his life to escape the feeling of not belonging. Now I stood there at the same point and said. 'I will no longer go on living *for myself...*'

Spiritually I was as dead as those who had taken their own lives; but having now died to myself, I belonged to the Lord Jesus, and I resolved to *live for him*, and to let him have his way in my life.

I still remember how the Bible spoke to me with the words of Christ: 'Look! I stand at the door and knock.' I replied, 'Lord, I am opening my door. You come in and take charge of my life and I will do only what you want me to.' That was my simple prayer, and I've never looked back! My life was in the hands of someone beyond myself. Prayer became real for me. I had peace. I was listening to God and living for him.

'Or being hated, don't give in to
hating,
And yet don't look too good, nor
talk too wise...'

CHAPTER

4

THE GENERASIAN GAME

EVEN WHILE I WAS STILL at college, the family pressure was upon me to get married. The fact that I found it difficult to strike up new friendships was immaterial. I didn't need to *find* myself a bride, one would be found for me, in an arranged marriage! I was facing one of the very biggest of cultural problems for Asians in the west.

I was at university studying for my PhD, about to become a highly qualified professional— and thus a good 'catch' for most Asian families. The word was out on the grapevine that a high-value, well-educated and very qualified boy was on the market. I felt like a prize-winning bull!

Some incredible offers of marriage came in, including one offering an annuity for life. I didn't need to work again as long as I married a certain girl who needed a socially-acceptable husband! There were some extraordinary dowries on offer but, for me, I just couldn't imagine marrying someone whom I had not got to know, and with whom I might not be able to interact intellectually and emotionally.

I wanted someone who would be a partner in every sense, and who ideally would also be a Christian. Yet I couldn't imagine myself marrying someone who was not from my own community. The dilemma lay in finding someone who would fit the bill, and whom I could meet in a non-arranged way. Yet every eligible girl would surely already be in the system and being presented with potential suitors. Somehow I would need to break the system.

The Family Way

My family is part of the Sindhi community—one of several thousand tribal gatherings in what used to be North India, and is now Pakistan. Though now dispersed all over the world, we continue to marry in the traditional style. The Registry Office wedding will be followed by a traditional ceremony which is a very colourful occasion. Marriage is a time to show off a family's wealth in the clothes and jewellery, the flowers, the musicians and the gifts to the guests—I once attended a wedding at which the bride's family had a baby elephant brought into the Grosvenor Hotel, Mayfair, to amuse the guests!

Sindhis encourage their children to inter-marry within the community. Should a young person seem to be veering towards an unsuitable marriage, steps will be taken to arrange a marriage very quickly.

To give an idea of the pressures that young people sometimes face, I heard of a young girl from the community who arrived in this country as a teenager. At school, her friends were the local English girls and when she began work she soon made friends with a male colleague. This friendship was sufficiently frowned upon for the process of arranged marriage with another member of our community to be put under way.

Her parents went off to Bombay to tap into the worldwide Sindhi network, where other members of the family had had matches made—though some had been able to arrange marriages to Sindhis within the British Isles.

As many Asian families know, there is a thriving marriage brokerage there, where families are introduced to other families that are compatible in terms of community of origin, caste, prosperity, etc. This girl had to give up her job, career, boyfriend, and way of life for a man who had been brought up in Morocco—a country very different from Britain!

The couple were married, because the girl's mother threatened to commit suicide if she refused to go through with the process, but at the time of consummation of the marriage, she fled back to her home in Britain. Later—after three years of agony and emotional crisis—the marriage was consummated and the relationship is a happy one; but what a way to start married life! The fear of stigma, and the network in which the Asian community operates, of course, kept all this hush-hush.

My own sisters are fortunately very happily married and live in Manila, Hong Kong, Marbella, New York, Poona and London. It's not so easy to keep in touch and I don't see them very often, though they fly in for weddings, and we exchange cards and occasional phone calls.

Nuts and Bolts

Whom does one marry? Westerners are unaware that in Asian arranged marriages, the rule is that one marries—not simply another Asian—but a member of the same caste and the same community. Living in India, you can be spoiled for choice. But with Asians dispersed throughout the world, it can be difficult for a family to locate a suitable partner within the same *country*, let alone the same town or the same street. Yet there are differences from city to city in the way things are done, understanding the travel system, knowing the unsafe areas, and being able to find the few shops which sell Asian food.

Traditionally, the girl's family pays a dowry which can vary from £100 to millions, depending on the wealth of the girl's parents—or how desperate they are for a suitor! The *size* of dowry can, of course, be a major source of discontent and rifts within marriages. It requires delicate and diplomatic negotiation, with family honour and reputation at stake. Trivial matters of protocol can cause immense ill-feeling: 'Don't they know that everything sent to us as part of the dowry should be covered in a red cloth?' For other families red is a taboo colour, and receipt of, say, a red sari taunts like a red rag to a bull!

The business class wants to marry within the business class, and the professional class within the professional class. It makes sense, because the new daughter-in-law will know all about the expectations upon her, and be able to handle the typical problems. Marrying across classes creates problems as mundane (but no less important) as the way food is prepared (should the tomato be put in the pan before the flour, or vice versa?)

Who runs the kitchen, and who cooks what, have probably been the downfall of more Asian marriages than any other reason. A new wife will find herself expected to obey her mother-in-law's whims about all things domestic. There are so many different ways of making chappattis, nans and curries that, if the new wife does not come from a very similar background, there will be immediate tensions as everyone else in the house begins to ask why foods they have eaten for years have suddenly begun to taste subtly different; and conservative Asian parents will never appreciate innovations within the kitchen.

A new wife begins on the lowest rung of the unspoken ladder of hierarchy in Asian family life, suffering the anguish of subservience and loss of identity. Even the children of the marriage take precedence. Husbands sometimes feel guilty that they are unworthy and have ruined their new bride's life with the loss of dignity they have heaped upon her.

It's not all negative, of course. There are certain advantages in arranged marriages, for some people. The families know and get along with each other, keeping to the same customs; bride and groom are spared the anguish and soul searching of wondering whether each potential spouse they meet on a date is the right one; the expectations of both parties are the same and there can be no misunderstandings; the two families form a closely integrated support structure which will help the marriage through times of stress; each side understands the same signals and the close match will minimise the risk of the marriage failing.

My brothers all happily submitted to arranged marriages, in Kenya, London and Bombay, respectively, but all to girls from the Sindhi community. These have all worked out well, through meetings with girls my family heard about on the 'marriage grapevine'—the dialogue between families of the same community which functions like an old boys' network. Yet the high rate of suicide amongst Asian girls between 16 and 24 years of age suggests that many arranged marriages are resisted in ways which have tragic consequences.

This Girl is Taboo

At a Diwali dinner-dance function, I met a girl named Sunita, a fellow Sindhi born in Britain whom I discovered was also a student, at the French Institute. I knew immediately that this was someone on a similar wavelength to myself and, though she wasn't yet a Christian, she seemed to know the Bible a lot better than me!

Now, I was on the committee of my college Indian Club, and I knew that we had some publicity material for a sitar concert that needed to be put up at the French Institute. I wasn't the publicity officer and it wasn't my job to sort this out, but I volunteered for the task. Phoning Sunita, I asked whether she would put up the posters, to which she immediately agreed. 'Great,' I said, 'you deserve a lunch!'

I think she thought lunch was too great a reward for simply putting up a poster but, of course, I was desperate to meet with her again, if my courtship was to bear fruit. As an Asian, she asked her parents for permission before meeting me; but, since this was a legitimate business lunch—very professional and all above board—they raised no objections. Thereafter we kept meeting, although—and most westerners would be staggered by this—in simply meeting socially we were crossing taboo boundaries.

'You learn how to present a situation to your parents so that they won't take offence,' Sunita remembers. 'Once my parents had agreed to Ram and I having lunch, I sort of assumed that future meetings would be okay. I didn't tell them any lies, but I didn't tell them everything either! It never occurred to them that I wouldn't tell them everything.

'It was two months, and several meetings later, that I went off to India with my parents for a family wedding. Ram sent me a lovely bouquet of red roses, and it finally got around my family that Ram and I were seeing one another. Then I went to his brother's wedding, and the news spread further.

'Before I met Ram, I told my parents that I wasn't going to have an arranged marriage. I was going to study, I was going to work, and would think about marriage at twenty-four. When the time came that I wanted to marry Ram, they threw it back at me that I was only nineteen, 'You can't possibly!' We got on well, and I liked him for himself. I'd known from the second time we met that we might have to get married if we continued meeting.'

After about three meetings, news reached a senior member of the Sindhi community of 'unethical behaviour by a young man asking a girl out', and 'does he realise the consequences'. I was 'summoned' by an uncle who carpeted me, and explained that I mustn't sully a girl's reputation by being seen out with her, or no one else would want to marry her. I had either to declare my intentions very quickly or stop going out with her! I asked her to marry me, and she—of course—had to consult her father...

There was a furore because I am from the business caste and she is of the professional caste. Most westerners will, perhaps rightly, say 'what's the difference?' Indeed there does appear to be no class difference between someone who works profession-ally at a responsible job and someone who runs their own business. Yet each caste chooses to believe that it is higher than the other.

People from each caste began expressing to Sunita and me strongly-worded views running down the other caste: 'Don't even step over the dead body of someone from that caste.' Neither family wanted the wedding to go ahead; each kept mentioning other potential suitors, but Sunita and I took no notice of these none-too-subtle hints. We were banned from meeting at one point, but accepted this stoically as 'par for the course'. Eventually the two families realised that we were determined, and reluctantly relented to our betrothal.

'My family were Hindus who accepted the fact that Ram was a Christian, on the understanding that I wouldn't become a Christian myself,' says Sunita. 'Ram said he would never force me to become a Christian, which they took to mean that I never would become a Christian, and that our children would be Hindus until they chose otherwise. In fact, I became a Christian of my own free choice two years after we were married.'

The wedding itself created tensions, because the two families just didn't get on. To the outside world, it would have looked like two Asian families at a wedding, but in reality the two families were not part of the same intimate community. We belonged to the same Sindhi community from the same town, Hyderabad Sind, yet within that one community there were differences which created anguish and anxiety.

The two families never came together in the usual intimate way, and have never really accepted each other, even after twenty years. When my wife and I were invited to family occasions, she found herself excluded from the cliques; it's subtle ostracism, which few people could spot from the outside. It's an endemic problem which is being carried through from first to second generations of immigrants. Asian families need to realise the consequences of their actions, and the detrimental effect it has on the family life that they so cherish.

Being in the west exacerbates the problems because there is now a much smaller pool of potential marriage partners, and choice is limited. Chances are that two young people of the same community and caste, living in the same city, will know one another from being blood relatives. Increasingly, the closeness of families who traditionally arrange marriages with each other's members is becoming such that only first cousins are close enough for a match, and then there is an increased risk of bearing handicapped offspring from such a consanguineous relationship.

It's hard for two people who have grown up knowing one another as relatives and friends from childhood to be suddenly told that now they are going to have to get married. The girl must learn to treat someone she had treated as a brother now as a husband. Muslim women often marry their first cousin, but it used to be far less common with Sikhs and Hindus. It's difficult.

Marriage Lines

In a *traditional* Asian wedding, bride and groom do not even meet until the wedding ceremony itself. In the west, patterns are changing to allow varying degrees of contact prior to the wedding, and certain freedoms in the choice of partner which would have been unthinkable a handful of decades ago.

There is the *modified traditional* pattern, where the young person has some choice in sifting amongst the names presented by the parents; though the final choice does not rest with the young person, but with the parents who hope to form dynastic links through a prudent marriage.

Then there is the co-operative *traditional pattern*, where the selection of potential marriage partners can be made by either the parents or the young person, though the eventual choice will be a co-operative decision in which the agreement of parents is the essential part.

In the *independent* model, the young person seems to follow the western pattern in making his or her own choice, but there is often a different emphasis: it is expected that the parents will be happy with the choice. In western families there may be a *hope* rather than an *expectation*.

The Stopes-Roe and Cochrane survey of Asian families in Birmingham (published as *Citizens of this Country*) showed that about a third of Asian young people are in disagreement with their parents over wedding patterns.

Seeds of Dissent

The researchers (Stopes-Roe and Cochrane) detected that 'the notes of discord crept into the comments made by some married young people, but powerful forces kept the family together... When the parents had gone to trouble and expense and many other people had been involved in the transactions, the young people recognised an obligation which they ought to accept.'

In communities where there is no escape into anonymity, it is doubly difficult to say 'no'; and there is further pressure where the would-be spouse has made a journey from the sub-continent.

'This is the second fiancé,' said one Muslim daughter. 'I sent one back because I didn't like him. Mum didn't like the first one either. The whole family didn't think he was good enough for me, so it was not just my decision—a family decision as well. But I couldn't send this one back, not really. People were talking—I couldn't do it again.'

Family support cannot safely be sacrificed lightly. Some consent to arranged marriages because, 'I couldn't think of a good enough reason to say "no".' The penalties of freedom can be high in terms of the reputation and social standing of families; in problems likely to face the discarded person; and the difficult alternative of meeting someone more suitable.

Though surveys show that young Asians are statistically less traditional than their parents, this is more likely to be the case when the background is Hindu, rather than Sikh or Muslim. Still, a third of young Sikhs and nearly a half of young Hindus expected a less traditional arrangement than their parents expected to allow them. Some foresaw trouble ahead.

Often a root cause is lack of communication between family members. In one family, the son thought his future wedding arrangements would be 'pretty liberal,' whilst his mother was adamant that 'the priest will decide. I have complete faith in him.'

There is often a sense of young people not wanting to step over certain boundaries and a fear (even in parents) that trying to transplant the arranged marriage system into an unfamiliar setting might prove a disaster. All concerned try to address the question: should love precede marriage, or follow it?

Mixed marriages between Asians and whites are another matter. There are several reasons against this: religion, family, communication, and children (half-caste children can have grave problems). Some consider it okay so long as it's the boy who marries the girl, and the girl takes the boy's religion for her own. This is perhaps another example of the double standard whereby it is seen as acceptable, even in the most conservative Asian families, for the boy to discreetly sow a few wild oats, but unthinkable for the girl—whose reputation must be protected at all costs.

Voices of Women

A girl wanting to marry outside her religion or caste is the traumatic eventuality which Asian parents most dread. It is a dire emergency which threatens them with social ostracism. No one will want to marry their other children, and if they go to Asian gatherings they'll be insulted and treated with contempt. Even their own relatives may not receive them.

The unthinkable is befalling more and more Asian families. Their daughters are becoming caught up with western lifestyles, following the route of women's emancipation and—unthinkably—burning their bras. In *Breaking the Silence*, several Asian women have written of their feelings:

'As an Asian woman I am in this country last 17 years. One thing I noticed, we are taken for granted: nice, soft and sari clad, timid little things... It is not going to be the same with next generation. They will question the expectation of them and want a clear answer.'—Manju

'I went through stages of wishing I was white so I could have more freedom to socialise with my friends. Being Asian seemed to me to be somehow undesirable... I have now lived away from home for three years and could never live at home again. I have come to enjoy the freedom and independence and responsibilities of adulthood which I am not given when I am at my mother's.'—Diljeet

'This is the present with the new generation, not the old generation.'—Nargis

As early as 1973 a YWCA survey showed that girls of Asian origin in Britain were 'existing at two levels and are inclined to question both to varying degrees. Unless they can successfully accept both they will swing from one to the other constantly, feeling 'stuck in the middle somewhere' as one girl put it, at a considerable cost to their confidence and happiness.' Asian women, even then, were beginning to speak their minds—usually in English, with a local accent.

'People come to a new country, they start a new life; but the past they can't forget it. They bring it with them—memories, attitudes and relationships,' says Shahida, a lady from Lahore (cited by Amrit Wilson, in *Finding a Voice: Asian Women in Britain*). Wilson laments that, in the nineteenth century, the British in India reinforced the caste system, placing it on a class basis, and did nothing for the role of women in Asian society. A woman with many daughters and no son is considered not merely unfortunate, but an actual carrier of misfortune...

A woman never belongs to herself; she goes from being her father's property to belonging to her husband. Subjugation, isolation and emptiness are commonly felt by wives in this position. When it is a matter of pride that women do not go out to work—though they can have plenty of work to do at home—loneliness can be a problem. In some situations, domestic violence can result from wives who cook or housekeep in ways different from those that the husband expects.

In Newham, a woman convalescing after a difficult birth, which had necessitated a forceps delivery, and who required extensive stitching afterwards, was approached for sex by her husband. He insisted on his conjugal rights, after which he left his wife bleeding, her stitches torn.

An extreme case of domestic violence occurred in the arranged marriage of the Ahluwalias, a coupling which was doomed from the start. Mr Ahluwalia came from Kenya, while his wife hailed from the sub-continent itself. He was a poorly-educated post office worker, while she was an arts graduate with ambitions to be a lawyer. Tensions from this mismatch flared into open aggression. He broke her finger in one attack, knocked her unconscious in another, threw boiling tea over her, tried to run her over at a family wedding, and continually raped her.

The violence continued in spite of warnings from Mrs Ahluwalia's brothers, and her promises to stop doing all the things he disliked, which included laughing, dyeing her hair, eating green chilli and drinking black coffee. After her husband threatened to brand her with a hot iron, she finally snapped. After pouring petrol over him while he slept, Mrs Ahluwalia ended her husband's bullying by paying him back for a decade of torment. Before dying of his burns ten days later, he made a statement to the police, which led to Mrs Kiranjit Ahluwalia's arrest and conviction for murder.

A Court of Appeal later accepted a plea of guilty to manslaughter on the grounds of diminished responsibility, and granted a retrial. Kiranjit was released after forty-two months' imprisonment, in a ruling applauded by lawyers and campaigners alike as a turning point for battered women who lash out at their tormentors.

Divorce

Not all marriages end in the extreme of one partner murdering the other. Lata is an Asian woman who rejected an arranged marriage to wed a man of her own choice, but divorced him five years later. She says, 'Remember girls, you are not alone and you need not suffer if you have the courage and strength and tremendous will-power, that is the key to success.'

Marital breakdowns caused by the pressures of extended families are not exclusive to the Asian community. Perhaps the most famous extended family of all is the British Royal Family. At the time of writing, the Queen's sister and the Princess Royal are both divorced, the Duke of York is heading for divorce, and the Prince and Princess of Wales have separated. The pundits have speculated that a major problem lies with the incompatability of royals marrying commoners who just don't 'know the ropes'. Perhaps this is the western equivalent of marrying outside your caste to someone who is not of the same community!

What of the future of Asian marriages? Another of those voices of Asian women comes from Dipa, who warns: 'If you bring a child up strictly, that child will run free at the first chance it gets... You have a life and feelings of your own. You have rights that shouldn't be taken away by any other person.'

Vibha left her parents' home, rejecting the Asian values for which they stood, and married a white man. 'I feel quite close to many things I have learned and assimilated in my life since I left the home of my parents. These ideas had begun to emerge as I protested vociferously in my own name and idealistic youthful ways against arranged marriages, dowries, poverty and social inequalities, the rich, the poor, the servants in the homes of the rich, Indian bureaucracy and the role of the state as I saw it then.'

Society and attitudes are both considerably different from a generation ago, but should this be described as *a way of life being lost*, or as *the chains of expectation being broken*? For those who consider the increased prestige of their family back in India where they send money and hope to return, perhaps the former is true; and for the twice-immigrant whose boats were long since burned, the latter. And what of the 'floaters' who don't know their identity, and are trying to avoid the shock of finding out? Though often versatile, they find it increasingly difficult to lead a double identity.

The jury is still out, but perhaps what is really needed is to take what is good from both Asian and western cultures, join them up, and create something which works for everyone. I'm speaking again of the Western Asian—a new breed who speaks Hindi with an English accent, and reads an Asian newspaper, *Eastern Eye*, which is published in English.

That way, disillusioned Asians don't have to torch themselves, and battered wives don't batter their husbands to death.

'If you can dream—nor make
dreams your master,
If you can think—and not make
thoughts your aim...'

CHAPTER

5

FAMILIES IN CRISIS

I T'S SAID THAT Ugandan Asians were expelled from their adopted land in an act of spite because a certain Asian widow, like most Asian widows, did not want to re-marry after her husband's death; a strong stance to take when your suitor is Idi Amin!

The despot's reaction was exactly the sort of eventuality of which the Asian community was most fearful. Any attack which is directed at the family—and particularly the womenfolk—fills the Asian heart with dread. We are very protective of our family life, and any absence of law and order which might result in women being assaulted or raped sends a tremor through the community.

Whenever African countries began to seek their independence, it wasn't long before Asian families in those lands—mindful of the turmoil which surrounded India's independence—began to look for properties in other parts of the world. All Idi Amin's actions did was to sharpen and accelerate a process which was already underway.

The only way in which the exodus from Uganda differed from my own family's leaving Kenya was the speed. Ugandan Asians had even less time to arrange for money to be taken out of the country, or to export their belongings. The rush for flights led to charter fares being callously increased to exploit the human suffering.

Idi Amin failed to understand that Asian families are very tightly-knit units which are difficult to marry into unless you 'fit' in terms of caste, community and background. The typical Asian home offers a constant stream of people to talk to, and no fear of physical isolation—though they are incompatible both with personal ambition, and with the increasing individuality of the age.

The extended family model is excellent for child rearing and for achieving goals in a family business, where it forms an essential economic as well as social unit; though younger family members are statistically less keen on the extended family situation than older members. For the British, the future belongs to the young, but the Asian treats the elderly with greater respect. Surprisingly, perhaps, as we have seen, daughters are often less traditional than their brothers.

Living with parents is a situation to be avoided, according to 90% of western couples, while 68% of young Asians and 87% of their parents think it's a fine idea. On marriage, the son stays within the family surroundings he has always known, but gains an extra companion, with whom he sleeps, while the daughter gives up the only life she has ever known, and may suffer an intolerable loss of freedom. Perhaps it is little wonder that Asian women want to 'rock the boat' a little.

Families at Work

Asians are happy with the idea of living with parents because of the emotional and material security in being together in a strange host community, but it's also cost-effective and economical. Many Asians do it to keep capital within the business, or as a way of saving up. It can be a competitive advantage that overheads don't increase as the family grows in size. When someone wants to get married, the family business generates the finance.

As I've said, it is a very Sindhi trait to want one's own business, and a Sindhi family is well geared to the task of running one. The extended families within a community often keep out competitors by acting like an old boy network. It's not unusual for Asians to expect one contract a year within the family to go to each family member's business. There is a closeness in a community where every family's roots go back to the same village of ultimate origin in Pakistan or India.

In the idealised Asian extended family, personal environment is tightly controlled. Even if someone wants to break off and set up a nuclear family or a business on their own, it's very hard because the entire wealth is tied up with the family, under patriarchal control. Even someone in their forties with children in their late teens will be under the control of the extended family.

The head of the household decides arranged marriages, controls networks of social contacts, and influences every aspect of family and individual life. A raised eyebrow or nod of assent keeps the individual under parental control well into middle age. Couples in their forties are unable to make their own decisions regarding their own children. If you break away and the patriach wants to be tough, you won't get your own share of the family wealth; indeed, there may be no liquidity in the business to *allow* an individual to take away his fair share.

Usually there are no legal agreements or wages paid to family members working in the family business, and no 'come back' in law. Everyone is equal and everything is linked. You can't break off without enormous loss, except in a devious way, and occasionally children will find a way to revolt. I've known cases of children in their twenties, totally trusted by their father, taking on a big deal, then turning the tables and kicking father out!

When it comes to inheritance, western laws are usually ignored. Those laws stipulate that where someone dies intestate—without leaving a will—then certain legal rules governing probate will apply. In Britain in 1993, for example, if you're married your spouse inherits the first £125,000 and the rest is split between the spouse and relatives. If you have children too, the spouse gets the first £75,000, plus interest for life on half the remainder, and the children share the rest. If you have no relatives, the government takes the lot!

But there have been cases in Britain where the families have simply (and illegally) applied Hindu laws of wealth transmission and inheritance. Here, everything goes to the wife, who is then expected to look after the children. When she dies, everything goes to the sons and to any unmarried daughters. Married daughters have had their dowries and are out of the system.

Typically the eldest son is expected to take control of the reins and behave in a benevolent way towards his younger siblings, through a system based on trust and family networks. This can be a problem when the eldest son is already a grand-parent, but unable to make decisions because the great-grand-parent always decided everything for the family! In practice, there are often clashes between the eldest son's children and their cousins. The tensions impose stresses and strains, due to misunderstandings that they have not been expected to have to think through. The family unit is a very powerful phenomenon.

Mind Your Language

When we lived in Kenya, our parents used to speak to us in the mother tongue and we would reply in English, resulting in bi-lingual conversations! It's common in Asian families in the west for those born in the host culture to speak the host tongue, while parents prefer to speak an Asian language. The Bir-mingham survey revealed the following striking pattern of lan-guage usage, which bears this out:

Language Used	Father	Mother	Son	Daughter
Mostly Asian	77.8	92.4	20.0	5.0
Both, but Asian from choice	18.5	6.1	25.0	43.3
Both, but Asian from necessity	3.7	1.5	55.0	51.7

The figures speak for themselves, with half the young people using their Asian language only when it is needed for communi-cation with other family members; though it's perhaps curious why there should be a discrepancy between sons and daughters *choosing* to speak Asian, with nearly twice as many daughters as sons making the choice.

Perhaps daughters are more keen to speak an Asian lan-guage from choice because of the need to please their mother, or in-laws. Ladies stay at home and, for daughters-in-law to communicate with their mother-in-law, they choose to speak an Asian language, in order to get along better with the matriarch.

'Choice', for parents is often based on speaking the language with which they were themselves brought up, as a matter of pride. In business, Asian men are more likely to speak an Asian language to other Asians. We can speak faster in it, and fewer people are able to eavesdrop.

Many older people might like to improve their English speaking and reading, but they feel that they haven't the time, or that they are getting too old. In not making the effort, many are unconsciously distancing themselves from their offspring, and weakening an already taut family life. They are in a difficult position because children can exclude them from a conversation simply by speaking quickly and fluently in a language they themselves understand only poorly; yet it is a language in which the parents actively desire their children to become fluent for their future prospects. It all adds to the stress pressing down on the Asian family.

Women in Crisis

Language problems are often the final millstone around an Asian woman's neck, weighing on the other pressures of living in a strange land, and leading to profound feelings of guilt and depression. If wealthy, an Asian woman may wear a beautiful new sari each time she goes out of the house, but it will often be a cover for inner turmoil.

Stress can lead to a desire for new things, in order to soothe the pain. This can create greed for possessions or status, which wrecks marriages. Some Asian wives feel their lives are dominated by the need to serve their husband's overbearing ego; by the sense of hierarchy around which an Asian extended family is constructed; and the sometimes claustrophobic nature of relationships.

Some Asian women are never allowed to go out of the house or to visit their relatives. It's like being in a prison and, if it's one of the tiny back-to-back houses in Bradford, where damp cellars are often used as living rooms, it can be a very harsh and unhealthy prison.

The conservative dress which some Asian women are expected to wear is an additional blow to the woman's self-esteem. The traditional *salwar kamiz*—baggy trousers and tunic, as it is sometimes regarded by its detractors—do little for a woman's sense of femininity. Nor does the *dupatta*, or shawl, which she must wear in traditional families, to cover her hair and hide the shape of her breasts, out of modesty. Many Asian women hate the dupatta, and wear it only at their mother-in-law's insistence. Many Asian women are happy to wear salwar kamiz in bright colours, but not in dowdy hues; while others resent not having the freedon to wear, say, a long skirt. Traditional clothing often has a symbolic and formalised significance which is irrelevant to the new culture.

If an Asian woman in Britain wishes to wear western clothing of her own choice, she may be regarded as a rebel. Denim and corduroy are particularly regarded as unsuitable for women.

One Sikh girl in Newham: 'The first time I wore jeans I didn't dare wear them with a sweater. So I bought a long top which came down well below my hips, to wear with them. I really was scared, the atmosphere became very stiff but nobody said anything.' A Sikh girl in Birmingham who wore trousers and T-shirt in the house was forbidden by her father from ever wearing them again.

The restriction on dress can be very awkward for Asian pupils and teachers alike, in schools where there is open contempt for anything traditional. One Asian teacher was made by her husband's family to cover her hair and wear a kamiz top over her trousers out of modesty—though, paradoxically, she was expected to wear a lot of heavy make-up too! Certain Sikh families are keen on their women wearing make-up, though Gujarati and Muslim families frown upon it. Conversely, Sikhs are often unhappy about their wives wearing saris instead of salwar kamiz, fearing them to be 'too modern'...

In the home, Asian girls are sometimes overworked and treated with little respect by their mother or their mother-in-law alike. In Asian families, members are often expected to hand over their pay packet—unopened—to the head of the household each week. A girl's dowry is sometimes made up of the money she herself has earned through her own work.

Sometimes the worm turns: Families of unquenchable materialism, whose women sail like bright galleons down the high street in their gold jewellery and richly embroidered saris, have been known to throw out their retired in-laws, seeing them as a financial burden. This would never happen in India!

Worlds of Prejudice

There are three types of pressure upon the Asian family in the west: those from inside the family; those from outside; and those which arise from conflict between internal and external expectations.

Those described above are internal *pressures. Let's look next at the* external *pressures, which fall into two categories: pressure from the environment; and implicit and explicit racism from people.*

An adequate home environment is a prerequisite for satisfactory family life, but many immigrants— and family members who visit from the sub-continent—are sometimes staggered at some of the inner-city slums in which some poorer Asian families find themselves housed. Even those living in well-to-do suburbs may not be getting a very good deal.

A study carried out by the Social Science Research Council of the cost and experiences of Asian households in owner-occupation in Greater Manchester revealed wholesale examples of racial prejudice. The home-buying behaviour of more than 400 Asian families was studied, along with a control sample of indigenous white families. The survey showed very little difference between the attitudes and behaviour of the two groups—save that the Asian households were paying an average of 5% more than the whites for equivalent properties! It's unclear whether this was because of bad advice, exploitation by the sellers, or simply poor access to information on properties for sale.

Another report, entitled *Black Council Tenants in Birmingham*, concluded that 'almost every aspect of Birmingham's council housing rationing system has, in practice, worked against black people: Black people are still grossly under-represented in council houses... Many blacks did not obtain housing in the areas they wanted... Lastly, the properties allocated were inferior in some respects to those allocated to white households of the same size, housed from the same quota.'

In Hackney, in 1983, a similar situation became so intolerable that the Council for Racial Equality served notice on the council relating to the poor treatment of immigrant families who were treated worse than an equivalent white family in similar situations.

The two main types of racial prejudice, according to Rita, an Asian woman living in East London (cited in *Breaking the Silence: Writings by Asian Women*) are 'the kind that is expressed in loud, explicit and often violent tones, the other a more subtle though no less expressive type... Phrases like "I don't think of you as being Indian, I mean you don't smell of curry or speak with an Indian accent".'

Amrit Wilson says, 'In Britain, the most brutal, and wide ranging racism which occurs day after day is not the work of fascist minority parties, but of Her Majesty's Government. It is racism written into, and demanded by, Britain's immigration laws. New black immigration has long ago been stopped, but any black man or woman who wants to bring dependents over, or be visited by relatives from home, is now afraid of what these people will have to suffer.'

Amrit tells of the horrors of immigration control, and the terrors of Harmondsworth detention centre in the arid concrete wasteland past Heathrow airport, with prison-like corridors, contemptuous attitudes, and inhuman rules. It's here that visitors or would-be immigrants are temporarily housed when there are problems about their documents or their reasons for being in Britain.

Amrit describes sixteen year old Shanez, sent to Britain in her bridal clothes and jewellery for an arranged marriage. She was held up at customs control, interrogated at Harmondsworth, sexually examined—in the 1970s, it was a routine part of investigation procedure—and taunted provocatively by immigration officials. White immigrants are seldom subjected to such indignities...

Pressures of Conflict

Conflicts between internal and external expectations are perhaps best examplified in issues relating to differences in east-west ethics; matters of sexual morality; and conflicting views on what is decent, modest and respectable.

'In my own life, the east-west conflict came to a head at Royal Ascot in 1966,' says Bina Sella. 'In the year of the birth of the mini-skirt, I was dressed modestly in a fashionable outfit modeled on the traditional Indian costume, the salwar kamiz. Coy about wearing a mini-skirt, I had opted for a Paris designed tunic in cyclamen pink with silver and black trimmings. The trousers were cut like knickerbockers, just above the knee. It wasn't a provocative outfit, though it was certainly a la mode. Several newspapers asked to photograph me for their fashion pages, in preference to the British models and actresses who, desperate to be photographed to promote their careers, had turned out in short skirts and tops with holes cut out, looking half undressed.

'After spending time in the Owners' enclosure—daddy had a horse running—we went through to the Bookies to place a bet. This involved crossing the Royal Enclosure, and there I was asked to see the Duke of Norfolk, whose job is to vet the clothing which is allowed at Royal Ascot. It was felt that the cut-off salwar kamiz 'shorts' I was wearing might fall under the heading of 'trousers'—which are banned in the Royal Enclosure.

'So this English aristocrat said to me, "My dear girl, if you take your bloomers off, you can go in wearing just the top." The top would have been like a very short mini-dress, and I would have looked quite obscene, so I refused. It was bizarre that a mini dress cut practically up to the waist could be regarded as more respectable than discreet trousers.

'From the number of press photographers who were there to record the incident, I think I was probably "set up". I still have the press cuttings, though most reporters failed to spot that the real story was an east-west issue relating to morality and decency. Only in Germany, one magazine took up the issue— pointing out that indecent women with their bottoms showing were allowed in, while a modestly covered girl like myself was turned away.

'The next day, I reverted back to my Indian heritage. I wore a sari and was allowed in. *I like my chips to be British, and my saris to be Asian!* The press got even more excited and I appeared, seventeen years old, on the covers of several national newspapers and television on every continent—in my sari. The incident was covered as far afield as Russia and Hong Kong, and still no one seemed to understand that a sari and salwar kamiz are equally Asian and equally respectable.'

Pressures arising from such cultural conflicts and misunderstandings are perhaps the most common, and are typified by the feelings of another Asian woman:

'At the age of fifteen, I suddenly began to experience certain emotional unheavals that one normally associated with people of that age. My feelings were divided: on the one hand, I was tempted to follow the casual lifestyles of my friends and at the same time I was compelled to stay loyal to the respectable Indian way of life of my parents.'

Relationships Prohibited

In a typically respectable extended family, if everyone works close enough to get home for lunch, the menfolk will eat together with the women doing all the cooking. Then the women will do the cleaning while the men take a nap, getting ready to go back to work.

Family life is lived together, with the desire to be together stronger than any desire to be apart, and the only time a husband and wife will have any privacy is after they have closed their bedroom door at night. (It has even been known for in-laws to intrude in the bedroom to make sure that a couple are 'doing it right'!) The couple might never speak to one another during the day. The Asian attitude is, 'What do you want privacy for?'

Any friendships, aside from perhaps a few superficial acquaintances made through work, are made through community channels. Typically, the head of a household will become friendly with the head of another household and, when invitations are given, they and their extended families will meet in a somewhat contrived gathering. They may all sit and stare at one another in a room, but that will be the uneasy nature of such a forced relationship.

It is hoped that romances may start to develop; but at the very first sign, the two sides will aim to convert this to an engagement very quickly, with a marriage perhaps a couple of years later, in order to protect the girl's reputation. There will, of course, be a shroud of stigma over the girl's family if the relationship is broken off. Protocol is very important.

Friendships made through work are allowed as long as they don't become anything more. At the first sign of romance, the traditional marriage process will be accelerated, bringing in other suitors in order to split the couple. Even same-sex relationships can be frowned upon, if the friend is felt perhaps to be of a lower-caste or a bad influence. Yet racial tension is often lessened at work when a racially mixed group of workers has a job to get on with day after day. Outside friendships are invariably on a lower level of importance than relationships within the family.

East and West

For my colleague Madhu, the transition to British life when she and her husband moved here from Italy was less traumatic than my own experiences. 'I went to a convent school in Singapore, so I had become acclimatised to the western lifestyle; we were never as Indian as many Asians,' she says. 'Whenever anyone asks us why we came to Britain, we say that we came for the sunshine, and that always gets a good laugh! Our real reason for coming was to be able to worship freely.

'My parents in law were very traditional and protective of their Indian culture. The workload was shared out and we found affirmation and support in most areas of life. But there were occasionally angry words and tensions—particularly about church-going. Each Sunday, we would never know until the last minute whether we would be able to get to a Church service, or whether some family responsibility would come up to prevent it. If we got there, I'd be trembling and shaking at the end of the service, worried that I would be home late. I wouldn't be able to get the meal ready in time, and the whole extended family would be kept waiting. There were situations where we didn't want to lie, but where the truth might hurt; parents would ask questions which I was expected to answer, no matter that I'm forty years of age.

'When we arrived in Britain, we suddenly found that we were taking far more decisions, from the very biggest down to the tiniest, and it's very tiring to have to think through everything. Relationships change, and my husband and I have suddenly begun to learn more about one another. I'm now the top of his list of priorities, and he's at the head of my list.

'I was used to being at the bottom of the pecking order beneath the aunts and uncles, and so used to having to wait for days to discuss something with my husband. Now we're both startled at the idea of being able to attend to one another straight away. The children have suddenly got more access. They used to ask me for things and a week or a month would pass before I could find the time to attend to it. Now we have no one to answer to, and things can get done quickly. There's a new found freedom, but it's traumatic too.'

Discovering each other in the fullest sense of the word only happens if husband and wife split off from their extended family to start out on their own. Children 'discover' their parents for the first time.

Finding someone to look after the children for a few hours can suddenly become a major task, when one has become accustomed to an abundance of child-minders within the extended family. Children become more critical, too, because their mother and father no longer have other relatives to hide behind, or on to whom they can shift blame. Madhu is now the one who has to approve of anything her children may want to do; she can no longer say, 'Oh, grandmother wouldn't like that.'

'There was, and is, still an Asian-ness about us; we have Indian names, wear Indian clothing and eat Indian food. Only now, we live in a nuclear family—husband, wife and children— instead of being part of a large extended family, with the approval and affirmation which comes with it. It's difficult because we are so used to having a large family around us, doing things together, and having the family's support.

'It's difficult in the west, too, because the young people seem to have so much freedom to dress and do as they please. It's *too* western, and *too* un-Christian, to my way of thinking. Their Christian friends find it easier to understand why I'm being strict about late nights. If their non-Christian friends feel that I'm being too restrictive, I tell my children that they can blame me if they like, they can just tell their friends that their parents are very old fashioned!

'My younger daughter goes to an all-girls school, so I am thrilled to bits. I was less worried about my son going to a mixed school, because it's a warm, friendly village school. When marriage comes along, I want them to marry Asian Christians. Once upon a time I would have said they had to be from the Sindhi community, but now I say "Asian will do", as long as they are Christian. There's nothing wrong in having an arranged marriage, as long as you can find the right partner. The biggest problem is finding such people. Are there any out there?

'Arranged marriages sometimes fail, but so do love marriages. The point is that, when love marriages fail, the parents can say, "Well, it was your choice." When arranged marriages fail, families suffer because the repercussions are felt through two often closely entwined sets of relatives. It's a bigger issue, and very embarrassing socially.'

Western Families

I bring up my children to live and work in Britain, in as English a way as possible, because they are first and foremost English. They need to recognise that they are Asian, in order to make allowances for prejudice. I'm not interested in teaching them about India or East Africa, but I do try to teach them the value of the family unit because, as a Christian, I believe it's a biblical principle. I explain the pros and cons of the extended family, which I think is a good system as long as the value of the

husband-wife axis is not eclipsed by family matriarchs and patri-
archs. Respect for parents is a good and worthwhile quality.

There is an Asian influence in the food we sometimes eat,
and they might see me occasionally in Asian dress. I want them
to be aware of their cultural heritage. They should not be afraid
of it, nor look down upon it. They need to find their own
identity, to handle racial tension, but not to over-react to it.
Whether they marry Asians or whites is of no concern to me, as
long as the person is God's choice for them. Prospective suitors
should be aware that my daughter will not come with a dowry!

Without Christ, there is a crisis, I personally believe. The
biblical pattern for families is for the wife AND husband to
both leave their families, to set up home together as a nuclear
family. Perhaps later, the time may come to take in bereaved
parents in their old age; but a couple initially need time to build
their own family identity, without too much intrusion from
parents.

There is a place, though, for a *biblical* extended family to be
worked out, with church members being 'aunties' and 'uncles'
and helping hard-pressed parents by taking on some of the jobs
which would be done by real aunts and uncles within an Asian
extended family. This should be a supportive structure, offering
someone to talk, share and reflect with, particularly over areas
of cultural tension, as difficulties arise. I believe that this is the
way forward for Asians in the west.

*Because issues have not been properly thought through in a
different culture, expectations in the traditional Asian home can
become overwhelming. The expectation clash creates a family
crash which can break up the home. Elderly folk are often left on
their own as youngsters break off and do their own thing.*

Suicides are the worst extreme in the chain of consequences
which arises from the desire of family members to marry outside their community. Girls run away because they cannot face
the prospect of an arranged marriage without love. There is no
getting over the social stigma. It's a hard grind, and why pay the
price?

Asians need to be open enough to admit that marriages don't
always work, and that families sometimes break up, without

there always having to be a stigma. These things are going to happen—forewarned is forearmed—but let's show compassion. Respect your children and don't give in to peer pressure. *It's not worth a death in the family!*

'If you can meet with Triumph and
Disaster
And treat those two imposters just
the same...'

CHAPTER

6

IN SICKNESS AND HEALTH

MRS PATEL HAD A TERRIBLE TIME. It was never like this back home in Bangladesh.

In the Canadian hospital having her fifth child, one of the nurses wanted her to 'take off her jewellery', referring to the ornate glass wedding bangle she wore, and which could never be removed until after her husband's death, when she would be expected to smash it off as part of the grieving process. All the doctors seemed to be male and—horror of horrors!—several of them had tried to examine her. She told them clearly, in Urdu that this just wasn't the decent thing for a respectable Asian woman to allow, but none of them seemed to understand her, and they weren't able to bring anyone who could. The food was terrible, she was expected to sit on a toilet seat used by others , and she couldn't even bear to think about what had happened once she had been wheeled into the delivery room...

It's a familiar story for many Asians in the west, whether it be in Canada or the Philippines, the Caribbean or the United States, Tenerife or wet old England.

British experts admit that, until recently, the National Health Service has given little thought or care for the particular needs of Asian patients, both physical and mental. McAvoy and Donaldson, in *Health Care for Asians*, suggest, 'there is a complex interplay between culture, migration, racism and men-

95

tal health. In addition, the presentation of psychological and psychiatric disorders is strongly influenced by factors such as culture, religion and language.'

There is now a recognised need for health care to be more flexible and patient orientated. Yet when Asians go into hospital, they are very often expected to fit into a routine which takes no account of their cultural needs.

One of the strongest of cultural needs is for female Asians to be seen only by female doctors. My own mother would never consult a male doctor. No way! Fortunately many health authorities and hospitals have now come to realise the anguish and embarrassment that is caused through being examined by a male doctor, and try to arrange for a female doctor, or at the very least to have a chaperon present.

Health visitors have gradually come to learn about extended family situations, to accept the hospitality offered in Asian homes, to relate professionally to members of the household through the patriarch, and to avoid discussing forbidden subjects—sex and contraception—with the family present. Most Asians are embarrassed by talk of sex, and Asian women are more modest than in the west.

Personal Hygiene

Personal hygiene differs greatly between the east and west. Most westerners think nothing of lying in a bath filled with the water in which they have washed, while Asians generally prefer to wash standing up and in running water.

Dental check ups are almost unknown in the east but routine in the west. Dental hygiene is often particularly bad in Asian communities, especially Bangladeshi, with severe dental problems requiring extractions under general anaesthetic at the age of four. Some health visitors believe it is possible that, because they see so many fizzy drinks and sweets in shops, immigrants think these must be good and have far too many of them. Asian families also display a tendency to keep children on the bottle for far too long, constantly bathing the young teeth in sweet fluids, which causes severe decay.

The routine which many Asians, particularly Muslims, have

of cleaning their nasal passages each morning by sniffing water up the nose and blowing it into a basin may be regarded as odd, or even repugnant, by westerners who may be alarmed by the noise it makes. The practice of putting coconut oil on the hair can cause odour problems which some westerners find offputting.

Many Asians do not believe that using lavatory paper alone is sufficiently hygienic, but prefer to wash themselves—always using the left hand. More lavishly equipped western bathrooms have bidets to make this easier. If not, remember that water spilt on the bathroom floor during washing might be mistaken for urine. It's best, perhaps, for Asians to use the western ways if you are a guest in a western family's home or in a hospital/ hotel, to avoid any misunderstanding or giving unnecessary offence.

Sitting on a toilet seat where others have sat is quite normal in the west. Squatting on the seat—as apparently many Asians used to do when they first arrived in the west—while avoiding contact with the seat, can damage the seat and dirty the lavatory. Cleaning the lavatory after use is regarded as normal practice in the west, though—of course—in Asian culture this task is reserved for those of the lowest caste. Doing it yourself, and learning to use a lavatory brush, can take some getting used to.

Asians traditionally use only their left hand when touching their sex organs, which can make the use of certain forms of contraception problematic. It is, for example, very difficult to insert a CAP with only one hand.

Hospital Care

In a hospital, the staff may not realise the serious significance of items of religious jewellery, a woman's wedding bangles, nose jewel, or a thread worn around the body. Neither may staff be aware of the seriousness to a Sikh of having part of his body shaved for an operation. Once these things are explained to a doctor or to nursing staff, they may come to realise that Asian patients are not being unnecessarily unreasonable. Oh, and Sikhs ought to know that some hospital authorities have been known to mistake the *kirpan*, or ceremonial dagger, for a dangerous weapon!

Hospitals can sometimes be an Asian's first real encounter with British food. Muslims cannot be expected to eat non Halal meat (i.e. meat from an animal that has not been killed in the prescribed Muslim manner) or pork. No one should be forced to eat on their fast day, but this will need to be explained to hospital staff. Hindus should not be presented with beef to eat, since the cow is a sacred animal; many are vegetarians, and most hospitals are now able to offer completely vegetarian diets.

Religious restrictions on diet can take a lot of explaining, but Asians need to make the effort when necessary, in order to avoid the appearance of 'just being awkward'. Many Asian diets can leave a patient seriously deficient in certain vitamins, and there may be good and valid medical reasons for taking mineral supplements—or for eating foods which would normally be avoided—if it means that you get well quicker.

I have an aunt with a thyroid problem caused by an extreme vegetarian diet. She was strongly encouraged to eat fish for a limited period, and a dramatic improvement in her health caused her to rethink her views on diet.

Patients shouldn't be afraid to ask someone to speak slowly and plainly, to repeat or rephrase what they are saying, in order to be quite sure of what is being said by medical staff.

Even when local authorities try to be helpful by bringing in translators to help Asians to make themselves understood, there is plenty of scope for confusion over which language(s) the patient speaks and understands best. Some think that all Asians speak the same language. Hindi and Urdu are, of course, closely related tongues—colloquial Hindi and colloquial Urdu are basically the same language. Speakers of these tongues may even understand much of what a Punjabi speaker is attempting to communicate. Bengali and Pashto are very different both from each other and from any other Asian language.

'If you don't know much English and you go to a hospital, doctors can be quite impatient with you,' says Dr Raju Abraham, admitting that he is guilty of impatience himself at times! 'Doctors feel that if you've come to this country you should know some English. First generation immigrants can get short shrift, out of irritation rather than racism. I know one consultant who used to tell me of a lady who had been in Britain for twenty years and still couldn't speak any English; how terrible!

'I thought once that a particular Asian patient of my own was not taking her tablets, but she didn't speak any language I knew, so I couldn't find out why. After discussing the matter with her family, I discovered that she *was* taking her medication, the medication wasn't strong enough, and a different course of treatment was required!

'Many Asians, when they know they're dying, want to go home to die; whereas most westerners would rather die in hospital. "Let us take him home to die, rather than letting it happen in an unfamiliar environment," say Asian families.'

Childbirth

Antenatal classes tend to be very unpopular with Asians, though many Asian women 'know the ropes' anyway through helping with sisters' and sisters-in-laws' babies. The language barrier may make classes quite meaningless, unless led by a bilingual female health worker. To persuade a woman to attend, western hospitals have come to realise the importance of explaining the classes to the whole family (in delicate terms) and particularly to the mother-in-law, since she has so much authority. Many Asian men, naturally, feel extremely uncomfortable at an antenatal session with women present. Good clinics will set up sessions just for husbands, led by a male health worker.

Asian women have gained a reputation for making a lot of noise during labour, though the opposite is usually the norm when Asian women give birth in the traditional way, at home within earshot of the rest of the household. It's not part of our Asian culture, but usually the result of pain and terror.

Whereas traditional Asian births are very much family matters, with all the female relatives present during the birth, but never the baby's father, in the west women most often give birth in a hospital with no relatives present—except perhaps the father! In Asian homes, a new baby is washed as soon as possible; but many modern hospitals are adopting the practice of handing the baby straight to the mother, to encourage parental bonding at the earliest possible stage.

'Instead of being in her own bed, surrounded by the women of her family in the privacy of her home, the woman delivers her baby in a technology-filled room attended by strangers, often men,' says Alix Henley. 'At some stage she may even be left alone. She has no idea what will be done to her next, or what she should do, and she cannot ask. Her fears can make things difficult for the delivery team, and any frustration and irritation they may show will make things worse.'

A translator and/or a female relative can help, but the hospital needs to be consulted well in advance so that arrangements can be made. (The same applies for any religious ceremonies which the family may want to perform after the birth.)

When my own children were born, I was expected to go in with my wife and help her with the breathing, but my brothers said, 'No, that's taboo,' they thought it would be too demeaning for an Asian male to do any such thing. Men are not seen to be natural carers, it's not macho! It's one of several stereotypes that are slowly being broken. Others are that housework and child rearing are a woman's work; the man earns the money, then comes home and watches television. Happily, more and more Asian men are taking the trouble to be present at their childrens' births.

When my second child was born, I was not living in an extended family by that time. I didn't know what to do about arranging care for my first child while going off to hospital to see about the new arrival. In extended families, of course, there would be other adults around, and the man would rarely be present at the birth anyway. The Church came into play, because a friend from my local congregation volunteered to care for my firstborn while I took my wife to hospital.

Though breast feeding is the norm in Asian countries, many British Asian women believe it is better—or 'more modern'—to bottle feed. It isn't! Breast is best, say the best medical authorities, though in the west women tend to wean their babies much sooner than on the subcontinent.

While Asian women at home would be expected to stay in bed for ten days or more, eat rich food to regain her strength, and remain 'ritually unclean' until her purifying bath forty days later, in the west new mothers are often expected to be out of bed within a few hours. She may exercise to get her figure back in shape—a bizarre concept to the Asian mind—might resume sexual relations with her husband within a few days, and be back at work within a few weeks.

Mental Health

Shock and withdrawal are often felt by women who have just arrived in the west, perhaps to join the husband to whom she may have been wed by proxy, and never met. Post natal depression, too, can be particularly acute in a strange land which doesn't yet feel like home.

Amrit Wilson writes of Manisha, a twenty year old Muslim girl from Sylhet, now living on a decrepit London housing estate. Her cry: 'My head aches all the time... Inside me sometimes is such anger, anger with my babies, with my husband, with the whole of my life. Then suddenly I am panic stricken... Late, late at night my husband comes home. He loves the babies. He is a good husband, but what can he do? And what can I do? How can I live, sister, how can I live?'

She was missing the enveloping love and concern she had known in Bangladesh, but now suffered from guilt and depression. Like many Asian women, she tended to rationalise her mental turmoil by describing it as an aching head. This anxiety transfer can also be described as the heart beating faster, palpitations, or just 'feeling low'.

In America, too, research shows that the extent of mental disorders amongst Asian Americans has been underestimated, because of the way expression of symptoms is influenced by culture. Asians were shown to express mental problems in terms of physical symptoms, or of feelings of anger, frustration, anxiety or depression.

Racism and exposure to contrasting cultures and lifestyles

has also taken its toll on mental health, with immigrants, refugees, the elderly, and women particularly at risk. Though the extended family can be a great help in coping with mental stresses, close family relationships and group-centred (as opposed to individual) orientation also *creates* interpersonal difficulties. Problems of personality and identity are exacerbated by cultural confusion. There is no indication, though, that Asians are more likely to suffer from psychiatric illness than Caucasians. Mind you, Asian mental patients would be screened out at the immigration stage. These days, an Asian with any suggestion of illness would not get a visa to come to Britain!

In one instance, an Asian woman—either through hysteria, mental disorder or through a cold calculated effort—resisted an attempt by her family to coerce her into an arranged marriage by completely cutting herself off and not speaking for several weeks. While in a medical unit, she lost her virginity to one of the other patients, as though trying to make it doubly difficult for her family to push her into an unwanted marriage.

Health Warnings

Jackie Rucker is a health visitor in an inner city part of London, where about 80% of the families she visits are from an immigrant background. 'Many of the Asian houses I visit are occupied by many more people than the white houses, because Asians live so much more closely together in their extended families. Asian homes in East London tend to have dark decor and simple furniture. Heavily occupied Asian houses make great use of sofa beds, with living rooms and dining rooms doubling as bedrooms at night.

'Because of the western climate, many Asians keep the curtains shut all day long and do not ventilate the house properly. This means they are not getting enough sunlight, and airborn disease can run rampant because of the lack of fresh air coming in.'

She has found that certain ailments are much more common amongst the immigrant population than in a corresponding cross-section of the population as a whole. Diabetes and cardiac problems tend to occur at an earlier age. Children have iron deficiencies, leading to anaemia, due to their eating patterns. Asians tend to turn up at accident and emergency departments at hospitals for ailments which ought to have been referred to their GP. Sadly, they sometimes turn up there with good cause; Asians seem to have a disproportionately higher number of accidents through driving poorly maintained cars...

Asians often cannot discern what is a serious illness and what is a trivial sniffle. Some doctors have reported the great difficulty this causes when trying to make an accurate diagnosis. Some act as though they are seriously ill when there is virtually nothing the matter, while one Asian woman complained of a 'slight pain in the side' which transpired to be acute appendicitis!

Jackie knows that it's important to treat each client as an individual. A plan of care and advice is often determined by the quality of communication. She sometimes asks how the particular illness is handled in India, in order to pick up clues.

She frequently finds difficulty in the translation of Asian tongues, even with a translator present. It takes time and experience, and she has learned that it works best when she can get eye-to-eye contact with both patient and translator. 'There's no real way of testing out whether what you have said has been accurately received and understood.

'The husband and the mother-in-law may have too much influence when the wife is the patient. Mother-in-law may disapprove of a couple using contraception, because she wants lots of grandchildren! I avoid this situation, if possible, by politely attempting to see the patient by herself, or by arranging a meeting elsewhere.

'In Asian families, a child's mother may not necessarily know even her children's dates of birth; that information would be found in the documents which the husband always keeps on his person, or locked away somewhere in the house.'

She finds that those born in Britain are more westernised in their health patterns. She is happy to report that, although she sometimes spots signs of wife beating, there seem to be fewer instances of child abuse than in western families as a whole.

Asians are far less promiscuous, particularly Asian women, so there is a far lower incidence of sexually transmitted diseases. AIDS is very uncommon amongst western Asians.

'Asian women are often much more experienced in dealing with babies, because they are more likely to have had experience helping sisters and sisters-in-laws with their offspring. Antenatal care is likely to be poor when a woman has come to the country part way through her pregnancy, but I find that the situation has improved regarding second generation immigrants. And fathers are now much more likely to be present at the birth.

'Asian men who have become widowed are much more likely to remarry than western men. They may well marry another woman from the deceased wife's family, and there can be quite an age gap, leading to many elderly fathers having second families.' One seventy-five year old man had a heart attack attending his baby's birth!

'What is going to happen when these elderly husbands die? Unless there remains a strong family support, there will be many young widows unable to cope.'

Health Administration

In the London borough of Newham, there is plenty of variety between the different backgrounds and social class distinctions. A middle class family from Delhi, for example, would have far greater knowledge of western health care than a poor Bangladeshi family. Those with a higher education level are more likely to be integrated, willing to be open to a health visitor's advice, and easier to get into group situations for health instruction. Bangladeshi women tend to be more submissive, and bound by their own culture.

Administratively, the naming systems that Asian families use for their children—and the great variety which vary from community to community—can often make it difficult for health workers to locate the right file, or to select the right set of medical records. The surname is sometimes the same as the father's first name!

The legal limit up to which a family is required by law to

name and register their child is 42 days, and Asian families—because they want to first consult relatives on the sub-continent—often wait till the last possible minute. For the first six weeks of a child's life he/she may not even have a name at all. Even when a name has been formally chosen, it may still change. Until named, a baby's records will be filed under the mother's surname—except that it is usually less confusing to speak of first and second names instead of Christian name and surname.

In practice, it's usually simplest of all for harassed medical staff to ask the parents for two names to write on the medical records and then explain to the parent that—whatever they call the child at home—these are the names they must always use for medical purposes. Patients with common surnames, like Singh or Patel, will be distinguished by date of birth.

'It's now our policy to immunise Asian babies at birth against tuberculosis, since there seems to be a higher incidence of TB amongst Asians, and the rarer forms too. Consanguinous relationships lead to higher incidence of handicaps and disabilities caused by inter-marriage between close relatives,' said one health visitor.

Newham, sadly, has one of the highest abortion rates in the country. Asians are far less likely to become pregnant outside wedlock—that usually only happens to good Asian girls in films, like the 1960s classic *Aradhana*—but there is a high rate of termination of pregnancies within Asian marriages where contraception has been erratic, and unwanted pregnancies have occurred.

There is an indication that some Newham doctors have tried to take advantage of ethnic minorities by charging them for items that should be freely given, according to a news item in the *Newham Recorder (16 July 1992)*. The local health authority has investigated a complaint that a patient was asked to pay for a home visit and for 'special medicine' for diabetes.

'Ethnic minority residents are afraid of going to their GPs to discuss contraceptives, sexual problems or their mental health because they think the doctor might tell their families,' claims a report by the *Newham Health For All* Group. Information in many areas of health was not available in community languages, and what information there was failed to take account of cultural differences. Much of it 'contains phrases and images which are predominantly white middle class,' states the report.

Jackie Rucker is keen to emphasize that it's not all doom and gloom. 'There are many Asian men who put themselves out to ensure that their wives get to clinics at the right time, and make their own arrangements for translaters when necessary.'

Raju Abraham bears this out, feeling that economic constraints sometimes prevent husbands from having as much time as they would wish off work to help their wives through medical problems and pregnancies.

The plight of Asian women in labour is perhaps a metaphor for the plight of the western Asian community, struggling with language, custom, prejudice, culture shock and alienation, to bring to birth a brighter future. As with education, marriage and family life, perhaps the next generation will be the one which finally gets to grips with Asian health problems, and conquers for good the difficulties of living in the west.

*'If you can talk with crowds and
keep your virtue,
Or walk with Kings—nor lose the
common touch...'*

THE BUSINESS OF EMPLOYMENT

I N MY COLLEGE YEARS, I completed my BSc (Hons) Physics degree, then realised that a career in scientific research didn't really appeal to me. Looking for a change of direction which would take me back towards the business sphere, a *Management Science and Operations Research* degree seemed a splendid way of bridging from physics back into business.

I registered for a doctorate in the subject, presented papers, but figured that if I really wanted to go into business, I'd better get myself a job sooner rather than later. I quickly found a job with Lloyds Bank International, in January 1976. For two years, I trained in finance, and gained the requisite qualifications from the Institute of Banking.

Eighteen months after my wife and I married, while I was still working for Lloyds, through the family network I came to hear about a better job, in Geneva. I remember coming back home after I'd been given the job and referring to 'my interview'. My friends had a good laugh. 'Ha ha, some interview.' There is no such thing as an interview when the candidate has married into an extended family. The family member is given the job and that's the end of it.

So in 1978, I moved with the family company to Switzerland, where the head office had recently relocated. The business grew very rapidly; it was a euphoric time for me. My innate skills were sharpened by the analytical training that I had received. The Geneva management team were soon handling a several hundred million dollar per annum turnover. The Group Chairman, Group Chief Executive and I worked very closely together. When the other two were away, I was in charge.

It was easier being an Asian in Switzerland than in Britain, because Geneva is an international, cosmopolitan town. Everyone spoke French, which I had learned at school. I needed some special night classes to brush up on the language, but I was soon into the swing. My three children were all born in Geneva, in 1979, 1981 and 1983 respectively. I lived in Switzerland until 1985, when I returned to Britain for a three month assignment, and I'm still here!

I was placed effectively in charge of the British division of the company. We made a number of acquisitions, particularly relating to the Scottish seafoods industry. It came to the point where the Chairman wanted me to build a world-wide seafoods empire, which took me back to India for a crucial trip—but that's another story which I must share later in the book.

Family Vocation

Most of my business knowledge has not been acquired formally; it was something I picked up from my father at the dinner table. I watched him, heard him, and took in the business skills he demonstrated. For example, when we were in Kenya, my father might say, 'A ship came in today and the owner had ten thousand Zimbabwean pounds which he needed converting into pounds sterling. The banks were closed, and he was eager to sail on the next tide, so I quoted an exchange rate and made 20% profit on the deal.'

The basic principle soon displayed itself: buy low and sell high. But the personal skill of one person convincing another that it was a good deal was the crucial factor, and I first learned how to negotiate by seeing how my father did it. If a potential client needed convincing that our family was able to fulfil a particular contract, he would be invited to our large and prestigious Kenyan home, so that he could see that he was dealing with people of substance.

I sat with my father when he was considering importing fashion shirts from London into Kenya. I saw how he assessed the size of the market, worked out transport costs, allowed for import duty, and calculated his mark-ups accordingly. He taught me how to send telegrams and to communicate effectively with the business world. Now, I try to ensure that my own children pick up informal business skills from me. The children will sit in when we have business associates round for dinner, so they have a chance to pick up how to negotiate effectively.

Being fluent in several languages is an asset because I am able to think in several languages. Learning a new tongue, if it's done properly, entails learning a new culture. It helps me to get into other people's skin, into other people's minds and to learn to think as they think. In business, that's a great help in surviving. I love the fusion, the richness and diversity that comes from being able to communicate effectively in several languages. But I *think* in English, and regard that as my mother tongue. Indian ways of thinking have occasionally led me most quickly to solutions, though this is true more in physics problems than in commerce.

I have always found business excites and thrills me. Though I trained as a physicist, the thought of experimental research gave me less of a kick than the prospect of wheeler-dealing. The excitement of physics came from the learning and, though I admire those who can spend endless hours in meticulous and painstaking research, such an occupation just wouldn't be 'me'. I've always been a trader at heart. The noise and the buzz at the heart of the business community was a powerful attraction.

Business expectations of Asians in the west are broadening and widening. Research in the Blackburn Asian immigrant community (published as *Transients, Settlers and Refugees*, by V. Robinson) makes the following assessment: 'Forces built into Indian and Pakistan society and family life encourage an overriding concern with status and a compelling drive towards achievement... The joint family system tranfers these ideals and responsibilities to the young members of the household whose energies are frequently harnessed to achieve these financial goals.' That means a lot of pressure on young family members.

In Search of Work

The Asian work ethos in the fusion culture of east and west, in which we find ourselves, is often more a rejection of Asian culture by those who were born and went to school in the west. Many highly-pressurised young Asian businessmen want to be as English as they can, even down to taking on English-sounding names. It's said that, however well qualified, an Asian name on an application form is less likely to attract a job interview than an English one. Some Sikhs cut their hair in order to blend in, and to increase their employment prospects. These can lead to heart-rending tensions within an Asian family and community.

There may be pressures, too, in figuring out how to avoid working for someone else, by being economically self-sufficient, and having your own little business which employs as much family labour as possible. Because of the benefits in terms of flexibility, cash flow and expenditure, a family business is a very nice little unit that's hi-jacking enough cash for the family to survive, and which avoids the embarrassment and stigma of social security support. As more family members come into the business, the competitive edge is sharpened. It may be a one-man business, with only one person there at a time, but—with, say, half a dozen people relieving one another every few hours—a shop can clearly stay open a lot longer than a non-Asian shop manned by the same person for the whole time it stays open.

The 'Paki shop on the corner' is now nearly as English as fish and chips. They employ Asian people because they understand the languages of the Asian community in the area, who support the shop because it is smaller, friendlier, and a 'little bit of India', as opposed to the sterile white local supermarkets. It can reach beyond just the Asian community, though. My father opened the shop on Sunday afternoons to serve white anglo-saxon Catholics coming out of Church after mass!

Hard Times, Hard Labour

Though many Asians have found rich business pickings in the west, the majority have humbler aspirations, and have settled for a steady income from often mundane jobs.

Many Asians come from a rural background—from one of the 4,599 distinct communities identified in India by 1991—where they were predominantly farmers. 'One of the many difficulties that such people face is the upheaval of moving from a rural environment to an urban and highly industrialised society,' says Patrick Sookhdeo in *Asians in Britain*.

'Further difficulties arise as men find their skills and trades unuseable and redundant in this new society.' Even doctors, teachers and engineers find their Indian qualifications unacceptable, and themselves precluded from finding positions at the level they had anticipated.

Desperate for employment, they find themselves in humbling jobs such as the clothing sweat shops on Whitechapel's Brick Lane. Once, when someone in my own family couldn't get a job, he worked illegally in a Bayswater restaurant. Apart from time on the bus, he was totally immersed in Asian culture, never seeing a white face from one day to the next, which hardly helped him to adjust to western culture.

Asian owners of clothing and textile workshops in Manchester used to bring in professional help from the white community. But the newcomers quickly realised that they would never rise to the top of the company because they were not family members, and soon left. There is now a tendency to want to send family members to college to acquire the relevant skills, though not many Asian families have achieved this.

Lower skilled Asians in Bradford go to work in groups, and spend the days working as a team. Employers see that this works well and allow Asians to 'cover' for each other when family commitments arise; they employ more Asians when the company expands; and they allow relatives to come to work and 'stand in' for family members. How this works in terms of National Insurance and tax I don't know! When Asians are employed in sizeable numbers by a non-Asian, there is a strong tendency to stick together. I believe these trends will begin to accelerate.

Asians want to get the best out of the economic climate, and to be protected as far as possible from any recession. Shops are secure, but they are hard work. Working for others can be less reputable, but a necessity in times of recession.

Disreputable Professions

Some professions are regarded by some Asians as disreputable at all times, while for other Asians it's almost disreputable to be in a profession at all, rather than in business for oneself, making money. The taboo occupations are those of cleaners and 'dirty' trades. The jobs that are disreputable vary from community to community; in some, being a hairdresser is regarded as normal, but in others it's derided and looked down upon. Being a funeral director is a taboo vocation amongst some Asians, and sometimes a worthy and worthwhile occupation amongst others—depending on the part of the Indian sub-continent from which you originate.

There can be severe family problems when a son or daughter wants to enter a profession of which the parents disapprove. The connotations of the theatre and film worlds, for example, are especially negative. Young girls might want to go for those occupations for the glamour, but parents are unlikely to encourage it. Jobs which necessitate the wearing of uniforms can be problematic in some families, who see uniforms as demeaning. Being a teacher may be acceptable in one community but not others. Even top notch lawyers can find themselves without respect in communities which value business skills and look down on professions.

At school, I thought at one time that it might be a good idea to join the Royal Navy and see something of the world; but my family quickly put a stop to that! It sounded very exciting to me as a 17-18 year old on the lookout for an alternative to university, if I encountered problems with getting a grant. I think I learned a good deal about salesmanship from the way the career was presented to me by the recruitment officer. In the end though, funding for higher education wasn't a problem, since I got a scholarship. I saw nothing wrong myself with a Navy career, though other Sindhis—including members of my own family—saw everything wrong with it.

It's important (though less important than in marriage) to have the endorsement of one's family in your chosen career. If the job itself is not very prestigious, it's always possible to cover up its deficiencies within the community by picking the right description. I know someone who 'works in journalism' who actually is attached to a pornographic magazine. A waiter might be described as 'someone in the hotel business'. A lot of that goes on!

Prostitution is always a disgrace, but titles such as 'a model' or 'hostess' are sometimes used to cover up. The Asian male can get away with murder, but the women must always be demure and respectable in communities where the double standard is a common currency. Secret strip shows in South London recently made the press, though it would always be kept very quiet within the community. Temple prostitution may be the norm in some parts of India, but socially, sleeping with a call girl is looked down upon if discovered.

The Spectre of Unemployment

Unemployment is another disgrace. Some Asians will even take jobs which pay less than the social security rate, just to be seen to have a job. Others work for free, with the extended family meeting the financial needs; Asians have been known to pay companies to employ family members, just to keep up appearances. Honour is all.

Unemployment in Britain is drastically higher amongst Asians than amongst the indigenous population. Take, for example, the experiences and perceptions of redundant textile workers in Lancashire during the early 1980s. Closure of textile mills left a 16,000 workforce on the dole queues. In some towns, 22% of those registered as unemployed were Asians, though Asians formed only 10% of the total population. Disadvantaged by poor communication skills, only 8% of a follow-up sample were able to find fresh employment during the 15 months of a survey.

A research project by the Commission for Racial Equality highlighted a gap in training provision for unemployed Asians, who are severely disadvantaged as compared with their white peers. Practically, they lacked the skills and industrial experience required for entry to the skillcentre training courses which would have equipped them for a new career.

Communication skills training needs to be wedded to vocational training in order to meet the distinctive needs of ethnic minority workers. Counselling and outreach was also recommended, together with 'open access' courses concentrating on technical skills.

In London, later in the 1980s, unemployed young Asians found it equally difficult to find places on Youth Training Schemes. Barriers to entry to training opportunities need to be dismantled and there needs to be positive discrimination in favour of ethnic minorities if widespread Asian unemployment is to be redressed. It is tragic when second and third generation immigrants who have no obvious difficulties with literacy or schooling are unable to make the most of their education, or to further their job prospects.

Back in the 1970s, when Ugandan Asians arrived in Britain stripped of their businesses and careers, many were forced to register as unemployed in order to secure money with which to feed their families. Only 21% of those interviewed by the Department of Employment kept their Ugandan job classification. One in three of those interviewed—many of whom had run their own businesses—were designated as fit only for unskilled manual work.

Some officers at resettlement centres seemed more concerned with their departure statistics than with good resettlement. If a head-of-household was offered a job anywhere in the British Isles, he or she was encouraged to take the job, find temporary accommodation in the community, and leave their family at the resettlement centre until they could find more permanent housing. Naturally, many families did not want to be separated, so resettlement and social absorption was a long drawn-out process.

By January 1973, 9,197 Ugandan immigrants (47.6% of the

total) indicated that they wanted to settle in London (this percentage had dropped by 10% in the previous two months) but only 75 homes in total had been offered by local boroughs in the whole of London! Many went to Wandsworth to join the thriving Asian community there; but they rapidly became dissatisfied with the dilapidated privately-rented accommodation and sub-standard living conditions they found.

In September 1992, 7,000 Somali refugees found themselves in a similar situation—'We are the nowhere people. We cannot go home and we cannot survive if we stay,' said one. 'I speak five languages, but can't get a job,' another complained. 'We left madness there only to rediscover it here,' said a third. None have permanent homes. How little has changed in twenty years.

It's difficult to find any job unless you have somewhere habitable to live, and it's difficult to find anywhere reasonable to live unless you have a job. This vicious circle has been perpetuated amongst many poor Asian immigrants since the moment they first set foot on British shores.

Employment Trends

More Asian women are getting into work, especially the widowed and divorced. I think this is because of loneliness and a sense of isolation. The role of the widow in Asian society is weak. She is not meant to remarry. When my mother was widowed at 21, she had the opportunity to remarry, but culturally she couldn't bring herself to do it—it was too great a leap. She has never worked in a job, living off a widow's pension instead. She could have worked at a career were it not a social taboo imposed upon her by Asian society. It's a tragic shame.

Fortunately, an increasing number of South Asian women are finding it possible to set up and run their own businesses. Despite her Muslim parents' protests that it was no job for a lady, Samina Saeed quit her job as a sales assistant at John Lewis, to become a successful fashion designer: 'My parents now approve of my work,' she says. Aisha Shaikh is the young proprietor of a dry cleaning company in Chigwell, Essex, while Sujata Jolly owns a beauty product firm and a health club in

Maidenhead, Berkshire. The stereotypes remain however: 'When I meet Asian men and I say that I am in business, they ask, 'Do you run a grocery shop?' complains Mrs Jolly.

At Heathrow airport, the people performing the menial work of sweeping, cleaning, portering and washing dishes in the kitchens, are often Asian women from nearby Southall, with perhaps a few Asian men for the heavier work. Asians are found at both the top *and* the bottom of the employment tables.

Figures from 1982 suggest that, at that time, the gross income of Asians of Pakistani origin trailed about 5% behind those of Indian origin, though those from Bangladesh were about 20% behind. Both Pakistanis and Bangladeshis were *twice as likely to be unemployed as Indians*, who were only marginally less likely to be unemployed than whites. This differential remained the same through to the most recent figures, in 1991—which actually average the previous three years' figures for greater accuracy.

The Labour Force Survey from spring 1986-88 showed that, although Bangladeshis featured prominently in the manual jobs bracket, Indian Asians have made considerable headway in professional and managerial jobs, and are actually more successful than whites:

Occupation	All origins	White	Indian	Pakistani & Bangladeshi
Managerial & Professional	31	31	34	28
Clerical	16	16	16	-
Other non-manual	8	8	7	-
Craft etc	16	16	16	16
Labourers	1	1	-	-
Other manual	28	28	25	41

(Source: Employment Gazette March 1990)

One of the reasons why Indians come out so well is that all forms of self-employment count as professional and management, and a much higher percentage of Indian men fall into this category than whites—27% against 15%—and mainly in retail.

In one of my current positions as a non-executive director of SOLOTEC (South London Training and Enterprise Council) I have begun to see the number of company directors from ethnic minorities begin to increase, not simply through more Asians building their own companies, but through achieving director status in other people's businesses. At a recent meeting at the House of Commons, it emerged that training grants are not being fully taken up by eligible Asians, so there is still some way to go.

The employment status of Asians in Britain is not all doom and gloom. Tariq Modood, in *Not Easy Being British*, points out that the 800,000 people in Great Britain who are of Indian origin, and who amount to 33% of all non-white people in the country (Pakistanis, at 17% are the third largest group, after West-Indians at 19%) have now achieved near equality with white Britons. 'They have for some years had an economic-educational profile which is much closer to that of the white majority than of the other non-white groups and may now have reached a point where, taken in the round, their performance is, or can be expected to shortly be, equal to that of white people.' This is racial integration indeed.

Perhaps the best sign that Asian businessmen have become accepted in their own right in British industry came in December 1991, when John Major celebrated his first anniversary as Prime Minister by hosting a dinner party at 10 Downing Street for Britain's Asian multi-millionaires, together worth a conservative £1.5 billion. Two of the Hinduja brothers were present, along with top Indian film star Amitabh Bachchan, Vijay Mallya (owner of *United Breweries*) and Naresh Patel, who owns *Colorama Films* and *Europa Foods*. The only businesswoman present was my aunt, Lakshmi Shivdasani (Bina Sella's mother) matriarch of the *Inlaks* group.

Dinner with the Prime Minister—who would have thought it twenty years ago!

'If neither foes nor loving friends
can hurt you,
If all men count with you, but none
too much...'

CHAPTER

8

WINDOWS ON THE WORLD

THERE CAN BE FEWER MORE effective ways of glimpsing a culture than through its music, literature and drama.

There are two distinct types of Asian music, the traditional or classic style, and the slushy Asian love songs popularised by film soundtracks. The top pop singers can fill the Royal Albert Hall ten times over—in fact, Lata Mangeshkar and Asha Bhosle have filled Wembley Stadium, and with high ticket prices.

Fusion music, mixing eastern and western influences with sitar, strings, tabla and saxophone, is new, exciting and different. It reflects the British Asian culture that is evolving. Just as the hybrid Creole French developed in French colonies, we are now seeing the westernising of Indian music, such as South Asian Concern's *Songs of the Kingdom*.

It's the same with arts and literature. We are starting to see English library books with Asian names, such as Riki, Ravi and Ram!

Asian Music

Music has social values and moral significance, in addition to its aesthetic merits. Indian music is based mostly on scales, while western music is strongly dependent upon harmony. Some consider that the melodies of Indian music faithfully express *internal* emotions, while the harmonies of the west reflect *external* emotions. Put another way, 'Harmony lets emotion in, and melody lets it out.'

Prajnan Ananda writes (in *Music of the South-Asian Peoples*) 'Indian music creates a history of its own with systematic and scientific evolution of notes and semi-tones, ragas and raginis, graces and aesthetic emotions, while western music weaves the history of its composition only. The nature of Indian music is to move around the drone which is its basic note. Indian music begins its movement upward from a fixed primal note and comes back to it after completing its circuit.'

A raga means something pleasing. As colour tinges the cloth, so combinations of tone tinge the mind. Asian music offers the notion that all music has its root in a supreme sound. It certainly offers greater freedom for improvisation than does western orchestral music—though perhaps less so than modern jazz or some forms of rock music.

Music, dance and drama originally sprang from religious performances. In medieval India, dancing girls used to worship the presiding deities with devotional classical songs and dance. Songs were seen as primarily devotional, and musicians as an asset to society, enriching culture.

Asian Theatre

In traditional Asian theatre, or *Natya*, the actors strive for total empathy with the audience. The *Natyasastra*, an ancient sanskrit thesis, supplies information about the function of theatre in society. Natya was originally given, it is said, by the god Indra as a pleasant diversion for the sudras—the lowest caste, who were banned from all rituals and services performed by the priestly caste, the Bramins—in the first millenium BC. Early Asian drama took the form of mythological tales.

Rangaraj, in *Natya Brahman*, says, 'The Hindus are an intensely religious race. Their religiosity is steeped in ancient myths and in complicated rituals that pervade every moment of their existence.'

Drama is seen as according with the order of the world, with its joys and woes. The theatre affords an accessible place for entertainment, but also for philosophy, history and other matters depicted in the dramas.

Says Anita Rangaraj: 'Theatre, thus, is not an ephemeral phenomenon—several hours of relaxation. It is as lasting as its impact, and vital in its existence as the universe itself... Higher orders of human endeavour are elevated stylistically in much the same way as Shakespeare elevated noble characters with verse and stylistic manner... Style, dance, music, poetry and acting are welded into an artistic organic form of theatre something akin to Richard Wagner's operas.

'The poet, the performer and spectator, each one brings in his own experience born of tradition and training to the theatre and it is there that they are fused into a single flow, a vision of Reality of the Natya-Brahman, the Theatrical Universe.'

Television and Film

The modern visual media have recently offered opportunities for Asians to express themselves in twentieth century electronic media and arts. Indian films are immensely popular, particularly those starring Amitabh Bachchan.

Asian faces are beginning to appear more and more on western television, and not simply on programmes like BBC's *East*, which specifically targets the Asian community, but as news readers, actors in soap operas, television presenters, sporting personalities, quiz show contestants, and all the other places where exclusively white faces were once seen. News reporting on Asian affairs often reflects a negative slant, though.

Time was when Asians were tossed a programme of our own at some hour of the day when most people were in bed; now, at least, *East* goes out early on a Friday evening, though Indian films are still only shown in the middle of the night! The television version of the Indian epic *Mahaberata* was shown in Britain in ninety-three episodes, with each episode first shown early on a Saturday afternoon, and repeated late the following evening. But, though an excellent introduction to classic Hindu literature, for me it was far too 'Asian'. By treating the story in its usual pseudo-historic setting, it came across as irrelevant to the modern world, so why claim that it was being shown for the modern Asian population? It probably appealed less to western Asians than to white British lovers of soap opera!

The BBC is currently going flat out to 'positively discriminate' in favour of ethnic minorities, in order to redress the balance. This is not something to which Asians are accustomed, so it's encouraging that 'No Go' areas are being liberated. We're still marginalised and there is no full integration; but, bit by bit, we're beginning to get there.

Asians are making their mark in the world of sculpture. Indian-born Anish Kapoor won the 1992 Turner Prize, in a field where, according to *The Daily Telegraph*, 'He is in a different league from the other candidates, not because he is, in the final analysis a *better* artist, but because his is an art of much more intellectual substance and moral weight. As in all his work, Kapoor tries to mingle eastern and western forms and ideas.'

Perhaps it is in the printed media that Asians are making the most headway. Salman Rushdie, of course, has won a trunkful of awards for his work; but newspaper journalists and editors too, made enormous headway in 1992. Two new Asian newspapers, both published in English, *Eastern Eye* and *Asian Leader*, now have certified national distribution where, only months earlier, the solitary Asian national paper was the Urdu *Daily Jang*. The launches respond not merely to fashion, but to demographic change. According to 1991 Home Office figures, 48% of the Pakistani community was born in Britain, and— with 31% under 16—the Asian community as a whole is one of the youngest, and most vulnerable, in Britain.

Songs of the Kingdom

As I researched the needs of the Asian community as part of a full time project for Spurgeon's College, where I've been completing studies for a Diploma in Mission, I could detect a cultural tension and alienation between young and old. I prayerfully felt that what was needed was a new type of music with a flavour that would express the new British-Asian outlook which is emerging.

My wife and I, together with talented young Asian musician

June George, produced an album combining classical Indian instruments and popular musical forms with lyrics in Hindi, Urdu and English. It's joyful new worship music, but I believe it is applicable beyond any religious context. Asian and western people of different faiths are asking for it on radio programmes not just in Britain, but in Tenerife, Marbella and even in the Middle East, Mauritius and Fiji.

One reviewer described it as 'a fascinating and lively mixture of eastern and western musical traditions produced by South Asian Concern, a multi racial group which seeks to encourage Asians in worship, spiritual growth and leadership. The result is a moving blend in English and Hindi of familiar worship songs with original material, with a distinctive and often beautiful musical arrangement.'

Another said, 'The tape brings together different layers of the British-Asian personality and different areas of that experience: the western instruments subserve a distinctly Indian musicianship.'

'There's no problem with music or worship by themselves, but these have led me to become involved in and to express some of the conflicts of the world,' says June George, who has appeared in the musical *Half a Sixpence* at Drury Lane, and organised a project called *Indian Summer* for the GLC at London's Purcell Room. 'In my own church fellowship, for example, I was aware that young Asians see things differently from their parents—and also from their mates at school who are not Asians—so we started using arts to express some of these experiences.

'In my last year at college, as one of my exam pieces, I asked all the ethnic minority students to come together to share their experiences. Some of the stories were incredible, so we used these to create a theatre piece called *A Question of Colour?*— and, you know, our white audience could not believe let alone comprehend the tensions which Asians and Afro-Caribbean young people go through, even in such simple things as language, dress and food.'

Contemporary Asian Arts

Born and raised in South London and married to Berley, also of
South Indian origin, June George feels that accepting an
arranged marriage depends on how much Asian influence there
is in a family. She has taken part in various arts festivals,
working with both a 17-piece Balinese Gamelan group and the
Isle of Wight Symphony Orchestra in one memorable concert at
the Medina Theatre.

'On a visit to India on holiday, I was asked to appear on
Indian radio and television, on a chat show called *Rainbow*.
Then I played the Gamelan (an Asian instrument) on the BBC
children's programme *What's That Noise?*. I've also performed
and arranged music for programmes on BBC Radio 2 and the
World Service, and composed and arranged music for two film
strips.'

In her local fellowship, music plays a very natural part,
though she finds spontaneous music-making seldom occurs in
South Indian families. June is interested and influenced by
music of all cultures—especially when they are fused. She finds
that many Asians, particularly from the northern part of India,
are extremely sensitive to rhythm, and require such an 'excellent beat' to dance to that the two styles just mingle.

In 1982, a pop song called *Ever So Lonely*, by Monsoon,
reached number 12 in the British single charts. Its evocative
fusion of Indian and western influences revived an interest in
combining east and west in ways which had not been attempted
since the late sixties. Bhangra music is now a thriving industry
within the Asian youth music scene, with its own record labels,
artists and video producers.

In Britain, it even had its own late night television programme, *Bhangra Beat*, for a few years around the turn of the
1990s, though this has since given way to a similar—though
broader ranging—programme called *Rhythm and Raag*. This
features Asian 'rap' artists, traditional Asian music, soul-jazz-
blues fusions, Indian dance music, and even Asian Reggae!

'It's interesting that Bhangra is geared towards the heavily
populated Asian areas, but those who live outside those areas
don't go for Bhangra very much,' says June. For her, violins

and saxophones feel much more comfortable than sitar and tabla. It was the need to break down the communication barriers between young and old that first led her to work with South Asian Concern on the *Songs of the Kingdom* project.

'It's nice to be able to create unity within the Asian community, and to be able to represent the way society is going. It all came together very easily, apart from the task of communicating with some of the Asian musicians. As a second generation immigrant, I speak no Asian languages. The music was very western but the time and budget didn't permit us to explore more interesting areas, or for me to get the Asian musicians to be more creative in the studio.' The first recording has succeeded commercially, so a second album should be available shortly after this book is published.

Religious Art

It must be clear by now that, for Asians far more than westerners, art often inextricably entwines with religious faith, and never more so than at *Diwali*.

Diwali is a bright festival of fireworks, pageantry, colour and spectacle, which makes a timely appearance at the end of October, to bring some much-needed cheer to those lengthening winter nights. Many schools in Asian areas mount special Diwali plays to celebrate the greatest festival of the Hindu religion, remembering and maintaining the Asian cultural identity.

Central to Diwali is the colourful story of Rama and Sita, which has provided many westerners, particularly school children, with their first glimpse of the fabulous world of Indian mythology. The story forms the crux of the cycle of legends found in the epic Hindu poem known as the *Ramayana*, or 'Rama's Way', composed somewhere between 300BC and 300AD.

Though the story exists in as many as seventeen different variations, some quite 'earthy', the basic story remains the same in each case. Rama is an Indian prince whose bride, Sita, is kidnapped by the evil Ravana, who sweeps her off to his island kingdom of Lanka. Aided by the monkey god, Hanuman,

Rama goes to the rescue. After various powerful demons are defeated, the tale reaches its powerful climax with the face to face combat between brave Rama, believed to be an incarnation of the god Vishnu, and the multi-headed Ravana. The 'baddie' is swiftly despatched and the lovely Sita—still chaste after her ordeal—is liberated.

Diwali has been called the 'Hindu Christmas' but, though gifts and Diwali cards—often portraying Hindu deities and containing sentiments such as 'Happy Diwali and a Prosperous New Year'—are exchanged, it does not commemorate the incarnation of any Hindu deity, much less any 'saviour of the world'.

Qalam Publishers have produced material examining the cultural and religious significance of the ten-day Diwali festival in the west within an atmosphere of respect. They comment: 'In some areas of India...touring groups of actors stage plays known as the *Ram Lila*. This concludes in a style similar to the traditional November the fifth bonfire night with huge effigies of Ravana, his evil brother and son, being burnt. Each figure is filled with fireworks and lighted by someone dressed as Rama firing a lighted arrow. The event can be witnessed in some public parks in the UK and is quite spectacular.

'With its colourful central story, Diwali offers tremendous scope for what might be called "education with a party feel." This is especially the case in primary and junior schools. Not unreasonably, schools serving sizeable Asian populations major on Diwali but the occasion is often developed substantially in locations with few or no Asian pupils. In an increasing number of schools, Diwali easily eclipses Christmas and Easter.

'Classroom activities depend on the age of the pupils but typically focus on the Rama-Sita tale. The basic story will be told and, using its characters and action, young imaginations encouraged to produce a variety of art and handicraft works. (Convention dictates that Hindu gods are coloured blue.) Schools television might transmit a version of the story plus film of Diwali festivals. At least one special computer programme exists to guide youngsters through the story.'

While children enjoy dressing up as gods, demons and

monkeys and stuffing themselves with food, many Asian young people celebrate Diwali with a Bhangra disco. Even Sikhs, whose faith is monotheistic, celebrate Diwali in honour of one of their gurus, Guru Hargobind, who lived in the seventeenth century.

Diwali's religious significance is often a source of concern to adherents of non-Hindu faiths, particularly Jews, Christians and Muslims. When they overhear remarks such as, 'Our Ravi is so excited, Mrs Shah wants him to be a demon in her class Diwali play!' they begin to fear that some sort of devil worship is being taught to their innocent young children.

As an evangelical Christian, I have to say that, though some schools have Diwali plays, *they can be more cultural than religious, and not something about which people of other faiths should automatically become alarmed.*

It can be alarming when Diwali eclipses Christmas or Easter, but perhaps the Church needs to rise to the competition and celebrate Christmas in an even more joyful manner. Evangelical Christians get needlessly worried about something which is primarily mythological, and which need not have any sacramental function. They can be essentially as harmless as *Macbeth* or *A Midsummer Night's Dream*, and considerably more harmless than the traditional western festival of Hallowe'en, which takes place at about the same time.

Nevertheless, world religions—and the world views upon which they are based—cannot be dismissed lightly. Religious intolerance is perhaps the worst prejudice of all, and a frequent source of anguish and family crises. We'll explore this strange world of faiths—more bizarre by far than western culture—in the next chapter.

'If you can fill the unforgiving minute
With sixty seconds worth of distance, run...'

9

THE NAMES OF THE KINGDOMS

FOR MOST PEOPLE IN THE WEST, Christmas is a time for giving and receiving gifts, getting together with family and friends whom you may not have seen for a while, eating and drinking a lot and generally having a good time. Many secular people lament that Christians have to bring religion into it!

Many Asians feel the same way about Diwali; but the celebration is based on principles established in Hindu religious texts—particularly the concepts of *karma* and *dharma*—which influence and are adhered to by nearly a billion Hindus. If it's just a play, then its fine, but if a priest is brought in to light incense, chant mantras and give the evening's secular entertainment a religious significance, then it's another matter altogether. Hindu priests are very few and far between in the west, and family elders will take on priestly functions as necessary.

When families leave their lights on so that they will be visited by the goddess Lakshmi, or by the spirits of the dead; or when companies have their account books blessed by a priest who signs them with the blessed mantra 'Om', Diwali has gone beyond any mere social or cultural event. It is dabbling in the unseen world of the spiritual forces.

As a child, I loved the *Holi* festival, a bright and colourful occasion celebrating harvest, where syringes of coloured liquid are squirted at you. You always wore your oldest clothing! Excuses for families getting together are always a good thing, so Western Asians treating these festivals as social functions seems okay. They can be great events, and good bridge building exercises.

A festival or celebration can transcend its original meaning and purpose. Christmas used to be a pagan festival that was renamed and hi-jacked into a Christian festival, with a different spiritual significance. As for Diwali, as a follower of Christ, I can graciously say it's 'a festival of light' and—if you choose it to be—it can be dedicated to Jesus Christ who claimed to be the true light of the world. This would be an immense help for those Christians who have come out of an Asian background, and who want to avoid ill feeling and pointless family feuds.

Young and old alike agree that religion is important, though many now consider that it is primarily only of social significance. Others say that religions are more than man-made structures, they are *spiritual kingdoms*, with the power to shape our lives and eternal destinies.

If that's the case, then culture must take a back seat. We must ask of any set of beliefs, not simply 'Is this culturally relevant to me as an Asian living in the west?' but 'Is this true?' and 'What implication does it have for my eternal fate?'

Hinduism

As we know, Hinduism has no founder, no creed and a variety of holy books, none of which claims final authority. It originated in India, and the majority of its adherents (perhaps 80% of the population) still live there. Though certain beliefs are common to all Hindus, other beliefs and practices vary from area to area. Even within a particular group, no two people necessarily view or experience their life or faith in exactly the same way. Hinduism is perhaps best seen as a related family of faiths than as one dogmatic and definitive religion. Hindus prefer to speak of it as *sanatana dharma*, the eternal teaching or law.

Though its origins are shrouded in antiquity, Hinduism goes back to the third millenium BC, at which point it was probably an *animist* faith—worshipping inanimate objects, seeing a divinity within them—though some consider that it may have begun as a monotheistic faith, believing in *Brahman*, the ultimate reality. But Brahman has normally been regarded as too abstract a concept to inspire worship, and usually devotion has been directed to one of the many thousands of lesser gods.

Around 1500 BC, India was invaded by the Aryan peoples, who brought with them their own pantheon of deities—of whom the most important were Agni, Indra and Varuna. This heralded the Vedic period during which the four scriptures known as the *Vedas* came together, being first written down around 800 BC. The most important of these, the *Rig Veda*, taught that the earth was created by the self-sacrifice of a being from whose body all material substances came to exist; and that the first man was Manu, from the parts of whose body the various castes first came.

A system of ritual sacrifice came about, which sought to emulate this first sacrifice through which the world came to exist. The problem was that (as H. W. Tull explains in *The Vedic Origins of Karma*) the death and destruction implicit in the original event created a situation for the sacrificer which would seem to have required the sacrificer to give up his own life: 'The Vedic ritualists attempted to circumvent this actuality by employing various substitutes (ranging from grain and animals, to a gold effigy) for the sacrificer's own person.' Phew!

The correctness of the sacrifice later came to symbolise good actions, or *dharma*, which could atone for bad actions, or bad *karma*. Around 800-600BC, the *Upanishads* interpreted this tradition to mean that a life filled with selfless activity is the correct way of using your god-given abilities, acting without desire for reward. These sacred texts also introduced for the first time—2,000 years after Hinduism first started!—the idea of *samsara*, or reincarnation. The immortal soul, or *atman*, must live hundreds of thousands of lives, over millions of years, in order to atone for the bad karma or bad actions committed in 'previous lives'; though the concept does not explain where the first man would have acquired any bad karma, if he had never lived any previous lives...

The Upanishads reflect the teaching of *yogis* or spiritual teachers who began to appear around 600BC to offer an alternative way of paying off the karmic debt—the Way of Knowledge, or *jnana*. This involves prolonged teaching and meditation in order to escape what yogis see as the unreality or illusion (*maya*) of everyday existence. Salvation, or *moksha*, takes place when the soul becomes completely pure, is released from all karmic debt, and becomes re-absorbed into Brahman. (This teaching emerged around the same time as Buddhism and Jainism, and there was considerable cross-fertilisation between the traditions.)

The next stage, which led to the development of classic Hinduism, occurred between 300 BC and 300 AD. This was the age when the epic legends came into written form. We have already discussed the *Ramayana*, which gives a focus to the annual Diwali celebrations; the second epic was the *Mahabharata*, part of which—the *Bhagavad Gita*—is perhaps the best loved Hindu text of all.

It presents a third path to salvation—the Way of Devotion, or *bhakti*. This is the simplest and most popular of the three paths; the one most practised by Hindus in east and west, in villages and cities. The follower centres his devotion on the god or goddess of his choice—Vishnu (and his incarnations) and Siva are the most popular—often using an idol or image of the god as an aid to concentration.

Hinduism also has a strong 'folk' element, with tribal deities, demons, spirits, astrology and many other concepts mixed in together. In the west, *hatha yoga* is used by people of all cultures as a method of exercise, though it has serious spiritual implications. *Tantric yoga* employs sexual practices and ritualised intercourse for occult purposes. Whatever methods are practised, the ultimate goal is to escape from the debt of karma, or sin.

Colin Bevington, in *New Light from the East*, writes: 'The significant thing about the philosophy of Karma is not so much the teaching of reincarnation, but the underlying implication that every man is the complete master of his own destiny. What he sows, he reaps, and the unending cycle of sowing and reaping continues with successive births and deaths as mere stages in the process, until through his own efforts, meditation or devotion his soul is liberated into cosmic consciousness, Godhead or Being. Man therefore earns his own salvation.

'But the Bible teaches that salvation cannot be earned, it is a gift (Ephesians 2:8,9) and that Christ is the only way for men to reach God (John 4:6). Man, in his one life (Hebrews 9:27) is answerable to God and not merely himself, for he belongs to God by creation and redemption, and even those who will not acknowledge this now will have to do so eventually (Philippians 2:10,11).'

God, in his love, has provided a way back to himself; but it is a way which many Asians reject without proper consideration, simply because it doesn't seem to belong to their own culture. They discard it simply to avoid a cultural conflict although, as we shall see, it is actually closely allied to Asian spiritual thought.

Sikhism

The Sikh faith originated in the Punjab, about 500 years ago, as a result of disquiet about Hinduism and Islam alike. The movement commenced as a group of disciples gathered around the Guru Nanak (1469-1539) to seek the presence of God. It eventually became an ethnic religion, where membership of the faith went hand-in-hand with living in that particular part of South Asia. It remains to be seen how Sikhism will survive when the community is dispersed around many western countries, each with rival and conflicting cultures and faith.

At its heart, Sikhism is a monotheistic faith—perhaps in reaction to the extremes of Hinduism, with its millions of gods—with God as the supreme teacher or Guru. If anything, Sikhs have returned to the old Hindu concept of Brahman, the ultimate ground of all being, and strive to understand what for millenia Asians have regarded as unknowable. Sikhs believe that God has revealed himself to humanity and that his divine and creative word (*shabad*) came to mankind in a distinctive way through ten historic gurus. 'Guru' is also a term applied to both the sacred scriptures, the *Guru Granth Sahib*, and to the Sikh community itself.

'There is but one God, whose name is true, creator, devoid of fear and enmity, immortal, unborn, self-existent, great and bountiful,' says the opening sentence of the *Granth Sahib*, a book I have read many times.

'God is one, the ultimate and eternal Guru (*satguru*), who provides enlightenment and understanding for the disciple who sets his heart on finding and serving him,' explains Douglas Davis in *The World's Religions*. 'In his transcendent state he is beyond description. But if he were no more than that, man would be unable to find and to understand him. Man would find it impossible to relate to a God without any attributes, so God manifests himself in and through certain phenomena which are known to man.... His grace enables sincere devotees to experience him through worship and meditation.'

Sikhs have succeeded in breaking down the caste system where they live, and they attach a great importance to community identity. Sikhism, like Islam, is a total way of life; but like Hinduism, it is acceptant of other faiths and creeds. When Mr Tara Singh moved to the Scottish town of Dundee as a small boy, his father sent him to the local Presbyterian Sunday school for religious instruction, in the absence of any Sikh temple!

Islam

Muhammad the prophet was born in Mecca around 570 AD. At the age of forty, he began to believe that he was receiving messages and revelations from God, which he was to convey by word of mouth, and which were eventually collected in the *Qu'ran*. The Middle East at that time was polytheistic, its dwellers worshipping many gods, while Muhammad proclaimed that there was but one true God, Allah—which simply means 'God' in Arabic. Eventually, and with bloodshed, the Prophet managed to unify the region politically, socially, economically and religiously.

Later military expansion brought most of India under Muslim control, under the Mogul emperors from 1556 until 1707, at a time when most Hindu philosophers (though not most ordinary Hindus) were monotheists. Islam was a benign cultural influence, in that it cut across the caste system. Largely because the faith was culturally contextualised, with new converts worshipping in Asian languages, about 12% of the sub-continent's population subsequently embraced the Muslim faith—though often keeping many of their old customs. Gradually, they have moved closer to standard Islam, a highly legalistic system under which the devotee must earn his own salvation by doing good deeds and having his bad deeds counted against him.

As Asian Muslims have moved to the west, bringing with them the spiritual kingdom of Islam, the demanding and cohesive structure of their faith has tended to prevent integration into western society. Islam restricts adoption of new customs and fresh ways of living, while giving rigid support to fundamentalism and the established ideas of its adherents. In contrast, while the precepts of Hinduism govern daily life, they do so in a manner less universally applicable, less rigid, and more open to change. Hindus like to live and let live.

Secular humanism is the common enemy of all faiths. Paul Hiebert writes of the increasing secularism that is taking place in South Asia: 'Traditionally, success in achieving secular goals provided people and groups with avenues to participate in the ritual sphere, which provided them with their ultimate status and identity. Today, secular goals in political and economic frameworks have become legitimate goals in themselves, and the basis for a new and modern identity.' (In *Religion and Societies: Asia and the Middle East.*)

Writing of Pakistan, in the same book, Munir Ahmed writes: 'Most Pakistanis still take Islam on trust, without ever understanding the meaning of words uttered in prayers, thus perpetuating an acquiescent mental attitude towards religious tradition, which is both uncritical and unproductive... It is only to be hoped that the increased spread of modern education in Pakistan will stimulate, in the near future, a reinterpretation of Islamic orthodoxy in the light of modern needs, and successfully bridge the gap between tradition and modernity.'

We are seeing faiths in crisis! Scholars agree that the future relevance of Hinduism and Islam to modern social life remain uncertain—even in South Asia, let alone in the west where so many Asians have now settled.

Christianity

Christianity is a monotheistic faith founded 2,000 years ago by a semitic Asian, named Yeshua, though he is better known by the Greek equivalent—Jesus. He certainly wasn't a pale-skinned European and, spending most of his time outdoors under a hot middle eastern sun, his naturally brown skin probably became a lot darker than the sallow skin of most Asians in the west.

Jesus was a good Jew who followed the faith of his ancestors, which involved a sacrificial system every bit as severe and demanding as the old Brahminic system. Both systems come up against the same obstacles. Both admit that man deserves to die for his sin, or karma, and look for a perfect priest to perform a perfect sacrifice that will atone in the sacrificer's place; and both are confounded because the priest doing the sacrificing is himself burdened with bad deeds and unworthy of the task!

Because Christ was the incarnation, or *avatar*, not simply of a lesser god but of the supreme God himself, he had no previous karmic debt. He was without sin, and thus an ideal sacrifice. The Bible describes him as a lamb without blemish, who made his one perfect sacrifice once and for all when he sacrificed his own body as an offering potent enough to take away, forever, all the bad karma of those who trust in him and put their faith in him.

'Such a high priest meets our needs—who is holy, blameless, pure, set apart from sinners, exalted above the heavens. Unlike the other high priests, he does not need to offer sacrifices day after day, first for his own sins, and then for the sins of the people. He sacrificed for their sins once for all when he offered himself.' (Hebrews 7:26,27)

Asian religious texts bear this out. In the *Satpatha Brahmanam* we read, 'Prajapatir yagnah'—'God himself is the sacrifice.' Tandya Maha Brahmanam of *Sama Veda* said that God would offer himself as a sacrifice and obtain atonement for sins.

The late Adhyaksha Mandapaka wrote, 'What is evident

from all these teachings is that the true and great redeeming sacrifice would be the one performed by the Sovereign Lord of this world, who putting on both mortality and immortality and becoming incarnate as God-man, would Himself be the sacrificial animal and offer Himself as a sacrifice to redeem mankind from their sins.' Mandapaka points out that the manner in which Christ met his death—bound to a sacrificial post with a *balusu* bush placed on his head, and nails driven into him—is fully in accord with what the *Rig Veda* says about the sacrificial animal.

Not only is the Lord Jesus the fulfillment of the Vedic tradition, he fulfills the yogic tradition too. To follow the difficult 'Way of Knowledge' requires a worthy teacher, or *guru*, who is able to lead you faithfully through to Moksha. He needs to be a true and dependable teacher, because there is so much at stake. The Brahmins have admitted their own uncertainty even on vital and fundamental matters like the creation of the world. Contrast the uncertainty of the *Rig Veda* with the magisterial authority of the Bible:

'Whence this creation has arisen—perhaps it formed itself, or perhaps it did not—the one who looks down on it, in the highest heaven, only he knows—or perhaps he does not know.' (Rig Veda) 'In the beginning God created the heavens and the earth. Now the earth was formless and empty, darkness was over the surface of the deep, and the Spirit of God was hovering over the waters.' (Genesis 1:1,2)

If your guru dies before he has led you through to complete liberation, you'll have unfortunately to start all over again with a fresh teacher, so it helps if your guru is also immortal! Because he rose again from death—and proved this by appearing to his disciples on the third day after his painful self-sacrifice—Jesus Christ lives forever as the eternal and true teacher or the *Sanatana Sat Guru* (The eternal one).

Because he has lived on earth as a man, Jesus knows all our weaknesses and temptations, and can identify with us completely. This makes him the ultimate bhakti deity, the God who truly loves us as we are, and who is supremely worthy of our love and devotion. Hindu deities help only their devotees, but

Christ loves passionately even those who do not love him! He intervened in history to walk the earth as a man who befriended sinners, healed the sick, fed the hungry and comforted the broken-hearted, as a perfect role model for his devotees to follow, then he died and rose again as the ultimate proof that he was indeed the perfect embodiment of the unseen God.

The Bible says: 'When we were still powerless, Christ died for the ungodly. Very rarely will anyone die for a righteous man, though for a good man someone might possibly dare to die. But God demonstrates his own love for us in this: While we were still sinners, Christ died for us.' (Romans 5:6-8) 'For God so loved the world that he gave his one and only Son, that whoever believes in him shall not perish but have eternal life. For God did not send his Son into the world to condemn the world, but to save the world through him.' (John 3:16,17)

The writer Adrian Plass sums up in beautiful child-like terms what this means to him: 'God is nice, and he likes me.' Followers of this kindly and benevolent deity spread across the globe after Christ's sacrifice and resurrection, spreading joyfully the good news to all who would listen. The disciple Thomas is known to have visited India in the first century AD, preaching the message of devotion to his deity as a means of Moksha. It may well be that his teaching influenced the writing of the Bhagavad Gita, which contains a closely similar message.

In the Gita, Krishna says to Arjuna, 'All those who take refuge in me, whatever their birth, race, sex or caste, will attain the supreme goal; this realisation can be attained even by those whom society scorns. Kings and sages too seek their goal with devotion. Therefore, having been born into this transient and forlorn world, give all your love to me. Fill your mind with me; love me; serve me; worship me always. Seeking me in your heart, you will at last be united with me.' (Bhagavad Gita 9:32-34)

This promise has been fulfilled completely in Christ. Lord Jesus told his disciples, not only that they would be reunited with him, but that he would graciously come and fetch them! 'Do not let your hearts be troubled. Trust in God, trust also in me. In my father's house there are many rooms; if it were not so, I would have told you. I am going to prepare a place for you... I will come back and take you to be with me that you also may be where I am.'(John's Gospel 14:1-3)

The Bible says: 'We are more than conquerors through him who loved us...I am convinced that neither death nor life, neither angels nor demons, neither the present nor the future, nor any powers, neither height nor depth, nor anything else in all creation, will be able to separate us from the love of God that is in Christ Jesus our Lord.' (Romans 8:37-39)

Salvation is by grace, or unmerited favour, and not by works, tantra, teaching, facility of mind, dharma, or yoga; indeed, scripture says 'All our righteous deeds are like filthy rags,' (Isaiah 64:6). Grace is costly. Take the story of the rich Asian woman whose young servant stole jewellery from her house and fled to Nepal, to live in luxury on the stolen wealth. When the money ran out, he returned home and was arrested. When the police asked the woman to press charges, she declined saying that the boy and his father had served her family well for many years and she would, therefore, forgive him.

Through this act of grace, the boy went free. But the grace that pardoned the thief cost the woman ten thousand rupees worth of jewellery. God's grace, given to us freely, cost the pure and innocent Lord Jesus an agonising death, nailed to a rough wooden cross, burdened with the karma (sins) of his billions of followers in every era and location. *He is the only one who has ever lived whose sinless life, and magnificent death, could repay such an enormous debt, and such a price surely makes him worthy of our highest devotion.*

Culturally, Christianity is a global faith, with adherents in every country on earth, including some 25,000,000 in India. Its message is universal. In contrast, much of Hinduism is culturally based, and truly relevant only on the Indian sub-continent. Of course, many of the ideas it contains are not even Indian, but derive from the Aryans, who probably came from the Baltic.

Wherever Christians are, in any country on Earth, 'Christ culture' takes supremacy. The Bible says that Christ's followers are no longer Jews or Gentiles, Greeks or Romans—nor, by inference, Asians or Westerners. All are one, in Christ.

Transformation

Before I became a Christian, when milk was spilled in the house, I would put a drop of it on my head as a sign of repentance in allowing milk, which comes from a sacred animal, the cow, to be carelessly spilled. I would go to the shrine in the house to light incense to Hindu gods, and regularly attended the Sikh temple.

That all stopped when I accepted Christ as my saviour, believing him to be uniquely the incarnation of the unseen God. The most difficult thing to stop was attending the *Gurudwara*, the Sikh temple, because they served very good free food! I used to worship at St Paul's church, Onslow Square, then get a bus to the temple, arriving at the end of the service, in time for a good scoff! It was *prasad*, food that had been offered to idols, but intellectually I rationalised it by remembering what the Bible says about everything being clean. These changes took time.

For me, the big thing was the release from all the idol worship, which had never seemed very fulfilling or satisfying, but which seemed to have a power and hold over me. I had feared, superstitiously, that if I didn't chant a particular mantra the correct number of times, that bad luck and ill would befall me. This was the ritual and superstition from which I was immediately released.

In my two years in British schools, Religious Education lessons and school assemblies were all above my head and I couldn't be bothered with it; but when I was presented with Christ's teaching later in my life, it struck a chord because of the unconnected bits and pieces of the Bible that I still remembered from my schooldays.

The biggest hurdle was coping as an Asian in the white church. It felt very 'heavy' no longer to be in the British Asian situation where I could be comfortable in two cultures. Instead, the pressure was on me from the church forcing me to make a decision for British culture, and to turn my back on my family.

This would be a hindrance for any Asian follower of Christ, unless they were desperate for an excuse to make a break, and I found it a tough time.

Now, there are some 40,000 Asian believers in Britain alone, and the joyful baptism of Asian Christians can take place in a context which allows Asian trappings to be present,—music from sitar and tabla for example. This makes it easier for non-Christian family members, Muslims and Hindus to come along as guests, and not feel too uncomfortable.

Some Asians accept Christ as just one more god or avatar to be placated and worshipped; but for me—perhaps because I was being told by Christians that Hindu gods were actually demonic powers and principalities—I stuck completely with Jesus alone from that point on.

When my mother asked whether I now believed that Hinduism was wrong, I remember replying, 'I can't say whether it's good or bad, I only know that Jesus said that he alone was the way, the truth and the life.' The 'Christ Experience' knocked all other religious matters into a cocked hat.

Conversion Crises

For a family member to change religion can be very traumatic for the whole family. For myself, I was a salesman and a diplomat, so I never consciously antagonised my family. I tried to show them the uniqueness of Christ which, for myself—from the peace he gave me—I knew to be very special. Praying to Hindu gods had given me partial peace, *but not the dynamic liberation from bondage, fear and shame which Christ bestowed.*

I didn't become 'abnormal' in any way. I pursued my career and did very well, so I wasn't a negative or antagonistic witness to Christ. I respected and lovingly obeyed my elders—except when they told me not to go to church.

My acceptance of Christ changed my attitude to everything else. I'd always had worries, and now it felt good to have release. At first, I didn't pray, other than selfishly! After I finally appropriated the power of prayer, faithfully praying for members of my family—whom I was careful not to antagonise—more than thirty family members have come to accept my Lord Jesus for themselves, one by one.

I was very fortunate to have had such a kind and understanding family. Fundamentalist Hindu families often kick out those who become Christians. I have a relative who came to follow Christ as a child and was immediately moved to an all-Hindu school in India. Satpal is another relative, from the East African Asian community. Since she became a Christian at college, she has experienced many of the same problems which I encountered.

'There were lots of pieces of my life that were not together. In church for the first time, I had tears streaming down my face, and I stood at the end when the preacher asked if anyone wanted to begin to follow Jesus,' she says. 'I didn't tell anyone at first, I was so frightened. When I eventually brought it up with my family, the arguments they presented against Christianity were forceful and I didn't have the knowledge to reply. My father kept saying it was a white religion, and that Indians have the oldest culture in the world.

'My mum used to catch me reading the Bible, and I would say, "Please bear with me, because I have my finals coming up, and reading the Bible gives me real peace." Now it's harder. Mother sees me as not being loyal to her. I try to explain to her, but she's given me a hard time over Diwali, because I said I wouldn't light a candle to the Hindu gods. My sister has been very antagonistic, after I used to be her closest friend. My family have threatened to disown me.

'Ram's help at this time has been a blessing. My father has now been to church with me—though he said it was a bit "over the top"—but my mother won't come. I hope she'll come when I get baptised. I can't turn back, because I have discovered that Christ is the essential truth, and I really love God.' Headway is slow, and every step needs to be carefully thought out if family unity is to survive.

The Good in Hinduism

Though I firmly reject the basic foundation for classic Hinduism—reincarnation—I continue to believe that the religion has much to commend it, and much that it can teach to Christians. The sense of duty, or *dharma*, that it advocates is still a useful concept, though coupled with culture it can be taken to extremes. Dharma in the sense of being a polite, law-abiding citizen doing your duty to the state must generally be an excellent thing; but young Asian women are sometimes brought up to believe that they have to keep on doing good, and if they can't keep it up they sometimes take the only way out— by taking their own life.

I like the idea of acting charitably, without seeking or expecting a reward, except that it can lead to desperate actions when Asians can no longer cheat the system to get the money to do their good deeds. I believe passionately that Asians need a faith that will unify families. Hinduism cannot do this because it's not cosmopolitan enough to prosper in the west.

Christians have a hazy concept of sin sometimes. They need to acknowledge their own sinfulness and meekly to ask God for forgiveness. Asians know all about sinfulness, or bad karma. This makes a better starting point for discussion than with someone who knows nothing of the concept of sin, but Hindus generally know nothing of God's forgiveness. The overlap in vocabulary can be used creatively to engage in dialogue. Once that starts, then the tension, anxiety and trauma that a change of religion creates in families can begin to be peaceably resolved.

Statistics show that Christians in America pray for only thirty seconds each day, and in Britain for about two minutes a day. My sister and her husband are devotees of the guru Radhasoami, and they meditate for an hour twice a day. Now that's a challenge for anyone, and it puts most of us to shame! Asian Muslims at college insist on a separate room in which to pray, but prayer sadly is often less important to Christians, who need to spend much more time praying sincerely, and meditating on the Bible.

Asians can also teach Christians about the awesomeness of God, a characteristic which is too often omitted from the teaching in many churches. There's too much talk about 'gentle Jesus meek and mild' and not enough of his divine sovereignty and holiness. Perhaps Hindus have a greater sense of God's awe through their acquaintance with the god of destruction, Shiva, devourer of demons and destroyer of worlds. Now no one is going to mistake *him* as being meek and mild!

'Yours is the Earth and everything
that's in it,
And—what is more—you'll be a
Man, my son!'

CHAPTER

10

A CHOICE OF FUTURES

IN APRIL 1988, I FLEW TO BOMBAY as part of a business trip
to buy prawns from the Indian sub-continent for the European market. I went around all the colourful ports of India
without so much as looking at what was around me. I focused
on the task in hand, visiting factories, boats and fishermen, and
all I did was talk about seafood!

On the last day, I met a group of Christian pastors who took
me around Bombay's shanty town, around the slums and
ghettos. I was absolutely devastated by the appalling sights I
saw. I couldn't believe it. The pastors told me about the so-
called 'slumlords'—imagine having to pay rent to live in a slum!
I saw child prostitutes, and five year olds—one of whom
reminded me of my own son—who didn't even have a pave-
ment on which to sleep.

During the plane journey back, in my first-class lounge, I
broke down. I just couldn't take the caviar and champagne that
was being offered on the plane. How could I be a Christian in
such conspicuous luxury, doing nothing about what I had seen?
Could I co-exist on the planet allowing a group of human beings
to live in the way I had just witnessed, while doing nothing
about it? I was faced with a choice of personal futures, and I
knew what I had to do.

Christmas Cracker

When I came back to Britain, I was determined to bring about a significant change. The first thing I did was to hand in my notice and give up my plush well-paid job. Soon after, I met Steve Chalke—another Christian who had visited the same site in Bombay and had also returned shattered by the experience. When we met, we devised a project called *Christmas Cracker*.

Steve Chalke had an 'Eat Less—Pay More' idea, a temporary restaurant where customers were invited graciously to pay more for less food—first world prices for third world grub—with all the proceeds going to famine relief in the third world. My business mind immediately thought 'franchise'! If hamburger chains could be nationwide, why not charity restaurants, set up in temporarily vacant high street shops borrowed from their owners?

Tea and coffee are the most obvious of all goods imported from third world countries. Each year British people alone consume 32 billion cups of coffee and 70 billion cups of tea— enough to fill 40,000 swimming pools. Little of the price we pay for our cuppas goes back to third world producers; but by buying drinks at our 'Christmas Crackerterias', much more of the money could be directed back to training and relief projects in poor countries. Christmas Cracker is not about doling out charity; it's not about giving a man a fish—it's about teaching him *how* to fish.

The desire at the bottom of our heart was not just fundraising, but to excite young people, make them aware of the issues faced by those in the not-so-well-off parts of the world, and help them to do something about it. The feedback we received from participating youth groups was that this was the best thing they'd ever done. They'd gained credibility and increased their profile in the community. It was a different kind of giving— young people's time and energy.

In 1989, *Christmas Cracker* was able to mobilise over 20,000 young people to create more than 100 temporary 'Crackerterias', raising £400,000 to help the poor people of India. It was the first relief and disbursement project in the west driven mainly by non-Caucasians. I believe that helping others is a natural instinct within every family—it seems so natural to most Asians to help others.

The *Financial Times* quoted me as saying, 'The creative use of business skills and links makes things happen. It gives me all the excitement of deal-making, not for making money for myself now, but for getting others excited, getting them to go beyond themselves—which is, after all, the reason that Jesus came.'

In subsequent years, we have increased to 400 restaurants at a time, with nearly a hundred community radio stations set up to spread the message to surrounding homes, drawing people to the Crackerterias. The *Daily Telegraph* picked up on the story and explained to its readers, 'If you want a record played, you pledge money. If you want to sponsor a programme, you can. This is a chain of neighbourhood stations, all given special restricted service licences by the radio Authority in the biggest single operation of its kind so far.'

It happens each year in the four-week run-up to the Christmas festival, and someone has calculated that a magnificent million man hours are donated to make it all happen. It's an example of what western Asians can set up to assist the needy people in South Asia. The total raised to December 1992 exceeded two million pounds.

For me now, true success is serving Christ. What is the advantage to a man if he gains the whole world but loses his soul?

Looking at the stories in the management magazines, I feel sorry for many of the people who have great wealth and riches. What use is fame, reputation or success when life itself is so transient? I was once asked of someone recently deceased, 'How much did the man leave?' I said, 'Everything.'

A successful person to me is the one who follows Jesus; a person who has given his life to the glorious Lord, who knows whom he is serving and where he is going when he dies. That is success!

South Asian Concern

On that fateful trip to India, I had seen poverty and felt called as a Christian to do something about it. Giving up full-time executive responsibility, I remained a non-executive director of the family company. I'm also a director of *The South London Training and Enterprise Council* (SOLOTEC), which keeps me closely in touch with local business. I live mainly off savings, pensions and some investments. *The Prince's Youth Business Trust* use me as an ethnic advisor. Christmas Cracker combines my faith with my business skills, but there is also one thing more.

I head up a small multi-racial group with a particular interest in South Asia. We are called *South Asian Concern*, and we encourage Asian Christians in the UK to support one another in earnest prayer and practical care. In this, we welcome Asia's rich diversity of languages, dress, food and traditions—but we reject the petty ambitions, racial barriers and inter-community suspicions that have marred both the UK and the sub-continent. We welcome partnership with Asians, Caucasians, and all who prize citizenship in the true nation of the future.

South Asian Concern (SAC) was formerly registered as a charity in March 1991, though it had been running as a concept for several years previously, since I met my fellow workers in the project Raju Abraham and Prabhu Guptara, and subsequently Dr George Dean and Ruth Bradby.

SAC publishes articles and newsletters; organises conferences and family camps; raises funds for developing countries, through *Christmas Cracker*; produces Asian music and videos; and sponsors relief workers in South Asia. It is an agency through which the problems facing Asian immigrants in the west can be discussed openly, the diversity and richness of different cultures can be celebrated, and the crucial issues raised in this book can be explored.

Summarising the Future

There are differences in the types and severities of pressures faced by different groupings of Asians, and we must be careful not to give answers which are too simplistic. Nevertheless, as we have seen, there are generally four options open to Asians in the west:

1 The tensions and stresses can be removed by wholesale assimilation into Western culture, though it won't bring ultimate peace. I believe for many it will create problems for later—perhaps as children want to discover their roots. But there are some who have happily walked away from their Asian origins without regret. Tara Singh, who arrived in Dundee from the Punjab, aged five, in 1955, is one example:

'I don't feel that I've experienced any problems as an Asian in Britain,' he says with a slight Scottish accent. 'When I was younger, I felt a bit different from the Scottish school children around me, but that's natural. If you go out looking for difficulties, you'll find them; but I think the problems exist only for a minority of Asians. The smaller the immigrant community, the greater the integration within the receiving community, and they don't experience the same clash of cultures.' They become white in all but colour.

2 A second option is for Asians to keep to themselves, or remain in ghettos, using colour as a uniform which gives a sense of identity. But this may simply be building dykes to hold back the inevitable tide, as futile as lighting a solitary candle to ward off the night.

There is no danger, if we open our doors and come out into the western daylight, that our Asian culture will suddenly disappear overnight. India would never have thrived as a culture without opening the windows for philosophical and cultural winds to blow in from all directions, without allowing the drafts and gusts to sweep her off her feet.

3 The third option lies in the creation of a new breed, the *Western Asian*. The version with which I am familiar is the British Asian, which takes the best of both worlds and creates a society and culture uniquely suited to the evolving needs of the Asian immigrant. Cultures are neither homogenous nor static; they are fluid. There has been a fundamental paradigm shift; young Asians want to identify with Asian culture, but they also

want the kind of independence which is taken for granted by people in the west.

The Western Asian is not necessarily born in the West, but he/she has lived here so long that western ways have become a part of him/her. The Western Asian will think nothing of having roast beef and Yorkshire pudding for Sunday lunch. He/she has no chip on the shoulder, wouldn't normally wear Indian clothing, but wouldn't rule it out either. Those born in the west may be used to school assemblies with Christian hymns and prayers.

In anthropological terms, the Western Asian is the focus point of a culture which is neither Western nor Asian, but a combination of the best qualities of the two. Cultural tension is inevitable as the frontiers are worked out and the possibilities and consequences explored, but the solution is not suicide or running away from change, rather it is finding hope and a vision for the future. You may first need to acknowledge the tensions and anxieties that exist in your own family, which are diaspora wide.

4 The fourth option is to sit on the fence as long as possible, but it's difficult to keep see-sawing between two cultures, being an Asian at home and a westerner outside. You can run yourself ragged to no good purpose. Better to seek a synthesis of culture where you can feel happy both at home and outside. The age of the Western Asian is dawning.

Warning to the West

The cultural wind blows both ways. Look, for example, at how the New Age Movement is taking in Asian ideas, like reincarnation; and they are there on television and in the cinemas too: *Star Wars*, *Star Trek* and *Masters of the Universe* have a very strong Hindu base, and soft porn movies like *Basic Instinct* have their roots in Indian philosophy.

One important concept which no account of the New Age has yet covered is that of *tantrism*—a Hindu philosophy which seeks to use sex as a gateway to spiritual experience. In the west, this finds expression in witchcraft where, in the Great

Rite, priest and priestess copulate—symbolising the union of the earth goddess and the horned god.

When creator and creation are seen as being the same, the basis of New Age *monism*, then not only is creation worshipped as being divine but also the procreative act—sex—is worshipped. Sex is looked upon as being a possible key to unlock the mysteries of the universe.

'Tantrism has a right hand path and a left hand path. The left hand side is highly destructive, but it is the right side which has succeeded in the west. *Tantrism is mythological pornography,*' Vishal Mangalwadi says of the sexual rituals in the tantric myths which the right hand tantrics believe are to be interpreted figuratively. Left hand tantrics in India enact them literally, to the extent of living in graveyards, abducting children and engaging in human sacrifices. This is said to give tremendous psychic experiences and powerful visions.

It is perhaps this goal which ritual child abusers seek to achieve in the west. Vishal believes radical feminism is influenced by left hand tantrism, which is making inroads in the west through the medium of the feature film: 'In the film *Basic Instinct*, the character played by Sharon Stone is like Kali, the Hindu goddess of destruction.' Those who say that western ideas have corrupted Asian values, ought to look at the windfall of pornographic ideas which have blown the other way!

Selective use of Hindu ideas is often dishonouring to Asian spirituality, since much of what is borrowed becomes distorted. It's all done in a very subtle way, but I feel that often the most frightening enemy is the one that doesn't look you in the face; which slowly and subtly takes over you and the culture in which you live. It will continue as long as Asians continue to bury their head in the sand and refuse to grasp the nettle of exploring *for themselves* the significance and relevance of their age old beliefs—and whether, perhaps, they lead on into a fresh *new* understanding of God—instead of abdicating the responsibility to New Agers who will use them often to selfish ends.

From Out of the East

Sociologist Milton M. Gordon has identified seven factors which measure the success of assimilation into a different culture. We've seen in this book that some Asians have made headway with all seven, while many others have turned them all around and created something new:

The assimilators have achieved for themselves (1) Changes of cultural pattern to those of the host culture, and (2) Large-scale entry into cliques, clubs and institutions of the host society. Within two generations at most, they will almost certainly have achieved (3) Large-scale inter-marriages, and (4) Development of a 'sense of peoplehood' based exclusively on the host society.

Those who are sitting uncomfortably on the fence will most likely become quickly either assimilators or Western Asians, while those who are anxious to retain a purity of Asian culture—usually those migrants who came directly from the sub-continent—will probably make the change at a later date.

Western Asians seem less concerned with the first three factors than with achieving: (5) Absence of prejudice, (6) Absence of discrimination, and (7) Absence of value and power conflicts. When these social evils have been conquered in the west, then we Asians can focus our attentions fully on relieving some of the problems of the third world. At present, it can seem as though the most intractable problems of the third world have come to the west with us, as unwelcome stowaways.

'Members of the ethnic minorities as a whole experience a number of social disadvantages to greater extent than other groups,' summarises my colleague Dr Raju Abraham. 'Their children are more likely to need special help in education. Unemployment is higher among the ethnic minorities than among the population at large, this disparity being particularly acute within the younger age groups. These difficulties have been compounded by the unfamiliarity with British society and, especially among Asian groups, by differences in language and culture. In addition to social disadvantages, there are also the effects of racial discrimination in certain areas of life.'

But, to quote an old Sam Cooke song, 'A change is going to come'. Like a train on the horizon, the rumble of its wheels

shaking the tracks, and the cry of its whistle bracing the night air,
the future is racing towards us—and it's going to be a rosy one.

Along with Afro-Caribbeans, Asians constitute the 'black' people whose struggle for equality is almost won; though it's amusing how, when Afro-Caribbeans proclaim black pride, and even a black 'hall of fame', there are never any Asians in it!

There are still some minority groups within the immigrant population—the Bangladeshis are a conspicuous example, as are Pakistanis to a lesser extent—who will still face the problems raised in this book well into the next century, but most Asian communities (including my own Sindhis) have made enormous headway. The current generation of Asian young people is probably the last that, on the whole, will have to go through the crisis of racial identity on the same scale. Language problems and unfamiliarity with western culture will soon substantially disappear and no longer be a barrier to educational and employment opportunities.

There are still tensions, and the problems are multilayered in their complexity. It's not simply a matter of Asian versus Western, sari vs jeans, or chappatti vs chips. The unfamiliarity of different cultures can be so great that like is not compared with like: older Asians may compare the best of Asian culture with the worst of western culture—which is as absurd as comparing a bright sari with a plate of chips!

Our title *Sari'n'Chips* emphasised the absurdity of some of the perverse reasoning and misunderstanding which still dog the immigrant community. But soon, it will not seem strange to see someone (perhaps even a white girl?) wearing a sari with a denim jacket, any more than it's odd to eat chips with curry sauce.

This is not an easy time, but giving birth is never easy. Perhaps the old poem by Rudyard Kipling, lines from which have headed each chapter, sums up some of the trials and tribulations, the hopes and aspirations that many of us share:

'If you can dream—nor make dreams your master;
If you can think—and not make thoughts your aim;
If you can meet with Triumph and Disaster
And treat those two imposters just the same...

Yours is the Earth and everything that's in it,
And—what is more—you'll be a Man my son!'

Life in the west can destroy you emotionally and physically, mentally and spiritually—but only if you let it. You can conclude that life is not worth the living, sit back and wait to die, or you can find the strength, hope and vision from beyond yourself to carry on and take your place in the struggle to build a new society fit for our children to live in, where prejudice and discrimination are things of the past. Then east and west will truly have met.

A Real Future

There is a hope and vision which some have found in the blessed Lord Jesus, the *Sanatana Sat Guru*. We don't have to become brown English people, to come to Christ; it's not just the white man's option. Some Asians call it *Christobakti*, and find in it a peace, or *shanti*, which passes all understanding. *Christ is the Boddhisattva who faithfully fulfilled his dharma, and whose merit in dying as the perfect self-sacrifice can fulfil our own karma, and allow our atman to return to Brahman, resulting in full and complete moksha.*

It's not a white, colonial, imperialistic option, it's as Asian as curry and chapatti! The Lord Jesus offers sonship and a place in God's extended family for all who follow him. Christ has been misrepresented to Asians, who have a serious need to explore Christianity in an Asian context.

When I became a follower of Christ twenty years ago, the strong message coming from the western church was 'you must become a brown Briton now. There's no room in the white church for Asian ideas, or for ways of helping Asians to acclimatise to western life.' Now, in the 1990s, there is more awareness of the development of church life on the Indian subcontinent itself, the development of theology in a culturally contextualised way, and the working through of pertinent issues. When I speak in churches, I proclaim loudly that it is possible to accept Christ while retaining your cultural identity. You can stay a brown Asian and still be a Christian!

South Asian Concern offers you the friendship, advice and support of fellow Asians who have found hope in Christ. It is a resource for you to use. Some need a confidante or advisor when faced with changing customs and personal identity. Write to me with your problems.

To discuss further the issues raised in this book, South Asian Concern is setting up forums throughout Britain and, soon, in other countries where Asians have settled. Write to me and I will put you in touch with people who can help. Write to me: Ram Gidoomal, c/o South Asian Concern, PO Box 43, Sutton, Surrey, SM2 5WL England.

An ending? How can you conclude something which is changing and evolving? This book has been an attempt to begin a journey which will not be completed in our lifetime. It highlights the problems of the Asian identity crisis, but the answers will vary from individual to individual, because everyone is unique in God's eyes.

May you find Him for yourself, and be enveloped in his perfect love. If you want to know more about how to be his disciple, please write to me *today*.

Selected Bibliography

Baqi, L. *Too Little, Too Late: Asian Young People and the Youth Training Scheme* (London YTS Asian Monitoring Group) 1987

Bevington, C. *New Light from the East* (Falcon) 1974

Crishna, S. *Girls of Asian Origin in Britain* (YWCA) 1975

Fearon, M. *No Place Like Home* (Triangle) 1989

Gidoomal, R. and Wardell, M. *Loving Your Hindu Neighbour* (South Asian Concern) 1993

Gifford, Z. *The Golden Thread: Asian Experiences of Post-Raj Britain* (Pandora) 1990

Henley, A. *Asian Patients in Hospital and Home* (King Edward's Hospital Fund for London) 1979

Kannan, C.T. *Cultural Adaptation of Asians Immigrants* (Self published) 1978

Kidman, B. *A Handful of Tears* (BBC) 1975

Kuepper, W.G., Lackey, G.L. and Swinerton, E.N. *Ugandan Asians in Great Britain: Forced Migration and Social Absorption* (Croom Helm) 1975

Lancashire Industrial Language Training Unit. *In Search of Employment and Training* (CRE) 1983

Modood, T. *Not Easy Being British: Colour, Culture and Citizenship* (Runnymede Trust and Trentham Books) 1992

Parekh, P & B. *Cultural Conflict in Asian Families* (Conference Proceedings) 1975

Prakash, A.D. *Fulfilment of the Vedic Quest in the Lord Jesus Christ* (Self published)

Prajnan, A. *Music of the South-Asian Peoples* (Ramakrishna Vedanta) 1979

Qalam Projects *Diwali* (Qalam) 1992

Rangaraj, A.R. *Natya Brahman* (Society for Archaeological Historical and Epigraphical Research) 1979

Robinson, V. *Transients, Settlers and Refugees* (Clarendon Press) 1980

Romijn, J. *Tabu: Uganda Asians, the Old, the Weak and the Vulnerable* (London Council of Social Service) 1976

Sookhdeo, P. *Asians in Britain* (Paternoster Press) 1977

Stopes-Roe, M. and Cochrane, R. *Citizens of This Country: The British Asian* (Multilingual Matters Ltd) 1991

Stow, P. and Fearon, M. *Youth in the City* (Hodders) 1987

Sue, S. and Morishima, J.K. *The Mental Health of Asian Americans* (Jossey-Bass) 1982

Taylor, J.H. *The Half-way Generation* (NFER Publishing Co. Ltd) 1976

Tull, H.W. *The Vedic Origins of Karma* (State University of New York)

Ujimoto, K.V. and Hirabayashi, G. *Visible Minorities and Multiculturalism: Asians in Canada* (Butterworths) 1980

Various. *Breaking the Silence: Writing by Asian Women* (Centerprise Trust Ltd) 1983

Various. *A New Start: A Functional Course in Basic Spoken English* (Heinemann Educational) 1980

Various. *Religion and Societies: Asia and the Middle East* (Mouton) 1982

Various. *The World's Religions* (Lion) 1982

Ward, W.P. *White Canada Forever: Popular Attitudes and Public Policy Towards Orientals in British Columbia* (McGill) 1978

Wilson, A. *Finding a Voice: Asian Women in Britain* (Virago) 1978

The Asian. Vol III. No 1.

The Holy Bible: New International Version (Hodders) 1979

Music from South Asian Concern

United in Christ, united in music.

Songs of the Kingdom

Although Jesus calls people from every nation and tongue, it is only recently that praise and worship music has begun to reflect the rich mixture of eastern and western cultural traditions. In *Songs of the Kingdom* Ram and Sunita Gidoomal of South Asian Concern and talented young musician June George have combined classical Indian instruments and popular music forms with lyrics in Hindi, Urdu and English, playing a variety of well-loved Christian songs. The result is a joyful new sound suitable for group worship or individual listening.

Available from Christian bookshops, or in case of difficulty from South Asian Concern, PO Box 43, Sutton, Surrey SM2 5WL. Each cassette costs £6.99 including post and packing (CDs £9.99). Please make cheques payable to South Asian Concern.

About South Asian Concern

We are a small multi-racial group of Christ's followers with a particular interest in south Asia (Afghanistan, Pakistan, India, Nepal, Bangladesh, Bhutan, Sikkim, parts of Tibet, Burma, Sri Lanka and surrounding independent islands like the Maldives.) Millions of people from these areas have now migrated to the west—1.5 million to the UK and 0.7 million to North America. Within these substantial communities there are many Christians. It is estimated that there are 35,000 Asian believers in Britian alone.

South Asian Concern encourages Asian Christians in the UK to support one another in earnest prayer and practical care. In this we welcome Asia's rich diversity of language, dress, food, and traditions, but reject the petty ambitions, racial barriers and inter-community suspicions that have marred both the UK and the subcontinent.

We wish to promote Christ's kingdom through an example of love and strategies for developing leadership. We long to see the good news proclaimed to all people by people from all cultures.

We welcome partnership with Asians, Caucasians and all who prize citizenship in the true nation of the future.

Some of our current activities:

- Publication of articles and newsletters such as *Asian Perspective*
- Organisation of conferences and family camps
- Fund raising events for the developing world such as *Christmas Cracker*
- Training on Eastern religion and the New Age movement
- Production of Asian Christian music and video
- Conducting seminars on strategic mission topics such as business management, Biblical counselling and cross-cultural partnership in mission
- Creation of a database relevant to Asian mission
- Sponsorship of Christian workers in South Asia

South Asian Concern, P.O. Box 43, Sutton, Surrey SM2 5WL
Phone: 081 661 9198   Fax: 081 770 9235